Whispers From Heaven

Linda Laybolt

Copyright 2015
By
Linda Laybolt

ISBN 978-1-940609-42-3
Soft cover

All rights reserved
No part of this book may be reproduced or transmitted in any form or by any means, electronic or mechanical, including photocopying, recording, or by any information storage and retrieval system, without permission in writing from the copyright owner.

This book was printed in the United States of America.

To order additional copies of this book contact:
Linda Laybolt
Port Colborne, Ontario
lindalaybolt@live.com
www.godsclub@weebly.com
Amazon.com

FWB

FWB Publications
Columbus, Ohio 43207

Poems

Visions Of Heaven

I have often thought about it, as you have too
What it is going to be like in heaven for me and you
I know the first person I will want to see is My Lord Jesus
And thank him for giving his life, to save all of us!

The pearly gates of heaven are mighty huge, so they say
Seeing them is going to be one glorious day
I've heard in order to get to them and pass through
You must know Jesus, and he know you!

They say the streets are paved with the finest of gold
They are always glistening and never need cleaning, so I am told
All that live here are dressed in the finest linens of white
White is God's symbol of purity, faithful and true, in his sight!

God has many gardens in heaven, with many flowers galore
This is one of his creations, that God so greatly adores
Looking up, you see exquisite shades of blue in the skies
With colorful rainbows, illuminating beauty to the eyes!

The choirs of heaven voices radiate throughout the air
Accompanied with the heavenly orchestra, can be heard everywhere
Angels sound trumpets and horns as they gently fly by
While the little birds sing in heaven, their sweet lullaby!

They say no pain, suffering or sorrows exist there
No one carries any burdens to bare
You won't see any tears, that is a thing of the past
Happiness here, forever will last!

You will get to meet all the people in the Bible that you read about
That alone will be such an honor, without any doubt
But the greatest privilege of all, will be meeting Our Lord Jesus face to face
And knowing that forever in his love , I will be embraced!

Linda Laybolt
Whispers From Heaven

Our Heavenly Father and Our Lord Jesus sitting on their thrones
Imagine seeing them together in their mighty home
What a glorious day, full of love that will truly be
Sweet are my visions of heaven, is all that I see!

The Rescue

To walk the distance seems way too far
To climb over the obstacles seems I'm not up to par
I need your help and guidance these days
I find it hard to see to walk through this haze.

I've walked so many paths and roads before
And never knew why till I reached the end what for
But this time, I don't know if I can make it at all
It seems as though I am up against a brick wall.

It almost seems like I've walked through the valley of death
Yet somehow I always managed through and caught my breath
But this time is way different than the others
I wonder to myself, will I walk through another?

Every bone in my body aches with pain
Something is different this time, something not the same
Before I knew I was going to get through
Because Dear Lord, I was walking with you.

After saying this out loud, I felt an arm go around me
I turned to look up and there stood, "He"
My Lord was smiling at me, telling me I'd be ok
And that I was going to see another day.

Today, my little lamb I will carry you
Because you're very tired, weak and feeling blue.

Linda Laybolt
Whispers From Heaven

The moral of this poem is we are never alone
The Lord Jesus never leaves His Flock On Their Own!

HOW GREAT THOU ART

My Dear Most Precious Lord Jesus, King of Kings
When I think of your love, my heart truly sings
Praise be to you, O Most Mighty One
Our Heavenly Father's, Most Divine Loving Son!

Obeying your Father, in Heaven above
You taught mankind, the true meaning of love
You walked on earths ground, spreading God's Word
To all in your path, who had not heard!

Sadly, they belittled you , mocking you time after time
But the love in your heart always, managed to shine
Persevering , never losing hope or faith along the way
Teaching God's Words on LOVE, completely devoted to convey!

The perfect man, innocent of all imperfections or sin
The one who holds the keys of heaven gates, upon to enter in

Persecuted throughout your entire earthly years, to the very end
Is a burden mankind carries, never being able to amend!

My Dear Precious Lord Jesus, it hurts my heart so
For all the pain and suffering bestowed on you, many years ago
If there was any way of changing and turning back the pages of time
I would have given my life for you, and begged, please take mine!

Why, Oh Why Lord, did they not realize the worlds loss
When they nailed the Son of God to an old wooden cross
Little did they know, you were here to save them
The true Messiah of the people, indeed you were Him!

Even while dying on the cross, your love still shined through
Begging your Father, "Please Forgive Them, They Know Not What They Do"
The precious love for mankind, you carried deep within like a gem
For The Lamb of God took away the sins of the world, with him!

Now in heaven, you sit beside Our Heavenly Father on a throne
My Dear Savior and King of Kings, forever, you will be known
My Precious Lord Jesus, I love you with all my heart
Forever, in praise my soul will sing "How Great Thou Art!

Forgive Me Lord For I Have Sinned.....

My heart cries out unto the Lord, forgive me please
For I have sinned again today, My soul is unease.
Everyday, I try my best to do what's right
But somehow failure stands in front of me by night.

It's hard to try and live one day without sin
When there is so much going on, within.
My heart cries out to those suffering and in pain
I feel their misery, something I cannot explain.

I see little children go hungry and I question why?
The world stands still with a blind eye!
Killings, rapes and child abuse occur everyday
The sky is blue, yet many lives remain dark and gray.

What pleasure do countries get going to war?
I get angry and ask is peace to much to ask for?
Homeless people live on the streets, in this day and age
People ignore them and my heart fills with rage.

Little babies get sent back to Heaven before they are born
Most of the world approves, but bitterness makes me scorn!
Mental illness patients are locked up, kept out of sight
Something else I cannot accept, it's just not right!

Linda Laybolt
Whispers From Heaven

Miracles take place everyday sent from Heaven Above
Yet, few give thanks to you, "Our Lord of Love."
It hurts me so to see you ignored, it trully upsets me
I get upset and think, Are people really too blind to see?

Yes Lord, In Your Loving Mercy I remain
I am filled with shame and remorse once again.
Maybe tomorrow will be a better day for me
I guess Lord, we will just have to wait and see!

Be Thou My Vision, O Lord Of My Heart

Be Thou my Vision, O Lord of my heart
Stay with me always, never to part
Guide me through the darkness, into thy light
Promise to watch over me, keep me within thy precious sight!

Be Thou my Refuge, O Lord, My Mighty King
Keep me close beside you, tucked under your wing
Be thou my great strength, when I can't go on
Place me in your loving arms, to rest my head upon!

Be Thou my Comforter, O Lord, wearily I cry
Gently wash away the tears, that shed from my eyes
Compassion is yours to bestow, so loving and kind
Warmth of your gentleness, flows peace to my mind!

Be Thou my Forgiver, O Lord forgive me, of all my sins
Teach me your righteousness, to feel love within
Meek and humble, your servant, I always will be
Surrounded by your love, I place my trust in thee!

Be Thou my Saviour, O Lord I pray
Your unconditional love you give, I'd never betray
Deliver me from this world of despair, home to be with you
Heaven is a place I long, for you to take me to!

Be Thou my Loving Father, O Lord Most Divine
Protect me from all harm, let me be Thine
Placing all my faith and trust in you, O Gracious One
Until the time comes, my work here on earth is done!

Be Thou my Redeemer, O Lord in Heaven above
Fill my yearning spirit, with ever-lasting love
Gracefully, Most Holy Lord, hold me close and tight
So I will remain forever, in your divine light!

Be Thou my Vision, O Lord of my heart
How Great Are Thy Wonders, How Great Thou Art!
Forever, being my first vision in my heart
May we always remain together, never to depart!

The Wooden Cross of Love

Three wooden crosses stood on Calvary Hill that day
Three wooden crosses for all to see, on proud display
Two common thieves, one to the left, one to the right
The one in the middle was God's shining light!

Innocent of all crimes, free of all earthly sin
With a love for mankind, he carried deep within
Nailed to a cross, the Son of God, just like the thieves
Two thousand years later, my heart still grieves!

Tears flowed that day by many, while others mocked and laughed
Not one person spoke a word of defense, on his behalf
All the good deeds he had done, seemed just to be tossed aside
Even knowing him, by some was completely denied!

All his earthly life, he held great compassion for everyone
But when he needed compassion most, sadly there was none
Abused by his transgressors, the Son Of God laid upon a cross
Hurting and suffering, his prayers, his love, never at a loss!

Linda Laybolt
Whispers From Heaven

Only a handful remained at his side, not willing to run and hide
They too were hurting inside, praying for his pain to subside
All eyes of heaven carefully watched and listened to their Lord
Cries of anguish from the earths angels, echoed for Jesus, whom they loved and adored!

There was so much sorrow and mourning, from Heaven that dark day
But it was something that had to be done, it was planned that way
Out of love for us and His Heavenly Father, The Lord Jesus came to us
Obeying His Father willingly, knowing in the end, there would be no justice!

The world received eternal life that tragic, mournful day
Forever, the image of the three crosses, in our hearts will stay
The pain and suffering that Our Lord Jesus went through
Was all out of unconditional love, for me and you!

So next time you see a cross, think of Calvary Hill
Think of Our Lord Jesus, think of the wooden cross of free will
Then say "Thank You to Our Lord Jesus", In Heaven above
Who suffered in pain for you and me, All Out Of Love!

FORGET ME NOT

My love for you is unconditional and never-ending
It has always been there, right back to the very beginning
Forget Me Not, that's all I ask you to do
For I have not forgotten you!

You are a very huge part of me although there are times
This, you cannot see
Creating you from dust of the ground, in my very own image
That's just the way, I wanted you to be.

Linda Laybolt
Whispers From Heaven

I gave the day full of light, along with the darkness of night
I gave you the sun and the stars
So with you, you would always see my shining light
I wanted everything for you to be perfect and right!

I gave you all that you see above you in the heaven's above
And gave you the earth to dwell upon, out of love
I sent my angels to guide and watch over you
I even sent you my only son, for the word of the Lord is right and true.

I gave you the Ten Commandments, in which I want you to abide
They are there for a reason and not to be tossed aside.
My Holy Scriptures were written out of love and tells all that is to be said
I gave them to you to understand me, each word I want,to be carefully read.

The greatest gift to you was the heart which I molded from mine
But I also gave you free will,it's your choice to keep it in the dark or make it shine.
A soul to you, I also gave and buried it deep within
A conscience was needed to let you know, when against me, you committ a sin.

When you need me, I will always there
For you know, I am the one who truly loves you and cares
Forget Me Not, that's all I ask you to do
FOR I HAVE NOT FORGOTTEN YOU!!!

Linda Laybolt
Whispers From Heaven

A Peek Through Heaven's Gates

Last night I dreamed I was standing in front of a huge set of gates
It felt like I was standing on air, for I could not feel the ground
I tried desperately to open the gates but they were too heavy for me to move
So I decided to take a peek in through and have a look around.

Then I decided, I better not do this
It's completely wrong, I wasn't brought up this way
So I stood there with my conscience swaying back and forth
But a small voice inside me kept saying, What is this place anyway?

Finally, I said I'm going to do it, I'll just take a small peek
So I got up real close to the gates without making a sound
I felt like a thief in the night, so scared of getting caught
It would be just my luck, of me being found.

The guilt hit me, I decided I better say a little prayer
Heavenly Father,I'm about to committ a sin, it's your forgiveness that I seek
I know it's very wrong, what I am about to do
So I'm asking ahead of time for forgiveness, it's only a little innocent peek!

My eyes must be playing tricks on me, for I could not believe what I was seeing
So many beautiful flowers, everywhere I looked beauty was to be seen
The colours were nothing like I had ever seen before, Where is this place?
I grabbed my arm and gave it a pinch, to make sure I wasn't in a dream.

The people here were all dressed in white clothes made from fine linens
Everyone here was so happy, for they were all smiling at each other as they talked
I could feel the peace and contentment that filled the air
Their souls were full of love as was the street full of gold, that they

walked.

Well I thought, could this be heaven, the streets are made of gold there
Don't be silly a small voice said inside, you just pinched yourself so you are very alive
Then I heard a voice call me by name, I'm so happy to see you, he said
I felt like a child who had just got caught, I froze but I really wanted to run and hide.

I turned around and there he stood with a glowing smile upon his face
I knew just exactly who he was, he held his arms wide open for me to embrace
I said I'm so sorry Lord, Can I ever be forgiven?
He replied, yes, my child, I planned it this way so you could have a peek of what awaits you in heaven!

The Angels Cried And Wept

Mankind committed the saddest sin ever
Killing the Son Of God will remain in our hearts forever
But it was meant to be as you all know
But the pain remains in our hearts from long ago!

We knew all along that this day was coming as foretold
For it had been written many times in days of old
None of us realized all the pain and suffering, you would go through
It was forbidden to interfere, there was nothing we could do!

We never left your side though it all, although we feel you thought you were all alone
In silence your servants watched their Lord be betrayed by the ones he called His Own!
Shame! We declared on the high priests of the temple! Shame on all of you!
You have dishonored your God in Heaven for all the wrong you do!

Linda Laybolt
Whispers From Heaven

Shame! Shame! On Judas for betraying you Lord
Shame! Shame! On those who betrayed you after you gave them God's Word!
Shame! Shame! On your own disciples who also betrayed you!
Shame! Shame! For all the pain and suffering, the Son Of God had to go through!

With all the screaming and shouting, it was hard for us to get near
But we did manage to see your eyes, were covered with sadness, but with no fear
We watched as the guards placed their crown of thorns upon your head
We watched as your beloved body was spit upon, beaten, mocked, crucified as you bled!

All of your teachings sent by their God, Our God, your Heavenly Father
Shunned and mocked on that day, Lest they forgot to Love One Another!
Hail! King Of The Jews, they mocked at you!
Let your God come and take you off the cross, were the words they threw!

As you laid on that cross, we watched in sadness and dismay
They say angels don't cry, but we all did that day
Heavenly Father wept as the tears flowed from Heaven
When you pleaded to Him that, they be forgiven!

Although you never complained for what they had done to you
We were all torn apart inside, for what you were going through!
As you lay there dying, darkness fell upon the earth
Not like the shining light that was given, at your birth!

This was the darkest day in earth's history that is known
The day the Son Of God, Our Lord was betrayed, by His Own!
But we your Heavenly Angels, never once left your side
For you are Our King, with you forever, we will abide!

Linda Laybolt
Whispers From Heaven

The love we feel for you is embedded in our hearts
Always, we remain your humble servants, we will never depart!
King of Kings of all the Heavens and Earth, Our Lord Jesus
Forever, your angels give praise unto you as you do, unto us!

In honor of the Angels who were at Our Lord Jesus side!

The Stairway That Leads To Heaven

As I sit here gazing at the great vastness of the sky
My mind reflects back to days, that have quietly slipped by
As you get older, some memories seem to fade
Just as the years that have passed by, are now many decades!

My childhood memories are embedded in my heart
Even though I am old now, they will never depart
It's like looking at a book, slowly turning the pages
When I think of my life, with all the different stages!

Alot of the paths I have followed, now I know were wrong
Some were short, while others were extremely long
All through the good times and the bad, year after year
Beside me you stayed, letting me know, your presence was near!

You have been so good to me, I don't know where to begin
Tears fill my eyes when I think of all the places you and I have been
You have and still are the biggest part of my life and my dearest friend
My love for you is like a bottomless cup, that forever flows without end!

As I reflect back on my life, I see things now, with a different outlook
My life with you has always remained an open book
Many times, I came to you for your guiding light
Many times, you've brought me out of the darkness of night!

Whispers From Heaven

I don't call on you for guidance anymore as before
My life feels contentment, what more could I ask for?
But as I continue to journey down this long old road
My steps have gotten smaller, with age I have slowed!

Looking through the book of my life, it's almost at the end
My Dear Lord Jesus, I need you one more time, to be my closest friend
As I look into the book, one more last time
I see a set of staires, that look hard for me to climb!

Will you be my guiding light of love, once more
Take me by the hand, and walk with me to Heavens doors?
The Stairway to Heaven shines bright with divine love
As is your smile as you reach out for my hand, to take hold of!

My Father's House

Everyone looked like they were dressed in their Sunday best
All in nice outfits except for the unknown guest!
No one saw him when he walked through the door
And no one knew or had ever seen him ever before!

He looked like some one from hundreds of years ago
He quietly sat all alone in the very back row!
The preacher had often said that in this place, all are welcome
But thoughts in everyone's head was where did this bum come from?

As the preacher began to speak, it was quite apparent
That he like the others, was full of dissent and judgement!
What right did this man have to come in here dressed like that?
Did he honestly think that we'd lay out the welcome mat!

There was a little girl who was sitting in from of Him
She kept turning around and smiling with a big grin!
Her mother said don't turn around anymore I say
That man should not be here, on this the Lord's Day!

The preacher said to himself, this is going to be a very short and fast service
He also as did his congregation, felt very unease and very nervous!
This was a church in a well to do part of town
So what possessed this bum to even think to come around?

They sang hymns of glory, they sang hymns of praise
The preacher spoke about God's loving ways!
The man in the back quietly listened to what the preacher had to say
But never bowed his head when it was time to pray!

The preacher was so happy, when the service was finally done
He stood at the doorway shaking hands with everyone, one by one!
The man in the back had not made any attempt to depart and go
He just sat there watching them walk by Him, with their heads hung low!

The little girl got out of seat and ran right up to Him, and gave Him a hug
I am so happy to see you Jesus, for you I do love!
Jesus looked at the little girl and took her in his arms, kissing her on the cheek
I love you too little one, you are truly my child, as you are the only one that would come to me and speak!

All eyes were on the little girl and Jesus now, then Jesus started to turn around
Even the preacher was too scared to move or make a sound!
Jesus stood up and said to them all, before he disappeared
In My Father's house, "All Are Welcome", you never who will appear!

A Prayer Of Love

Take my hand, hold it tight within yours
Shine your light of love, upon me forevermore
Stay close beside me, protect me from all harm
Be my refuge, safe within your arms!

Linda Laybolt
Whispers From Heaven

Keep me within your sight, always within full view
The road of righteousness is the road that I must pursue!
For I am not perfect, sin is hiding behind every turn
I don't want to step on a path, that leads to no return!

For there will be times, that I will stray
Those are the times, I need you to find my way
Stay with me through this life, each and every day
Wrapped within your love, don't ever go away!

You are my foundation, my rock that I lean on
You are my strength, when called upon
Pick me up when I stumble and fall, rescue me
When darkness falls, be my guiding light, for me to see!

My life is yours, I give it willingly to you
Your unconditional love is all I need, to see me through
Holy, Holy, Holy, Lord God Almighty
What was, is and is to come! Forever, I will love thee!

The Last Road

He said, I'm ready to come Lord with you
I'm weary and tired, what else is there left for me to do?
I'm old and all alone, I can't walk another road
My burdens are too heavy, I cannot carry the load.

You and I have travelled so many paths to the end
Each time becoming closer, now you are my best friend!
I've lived my life to the best that I could
Unto others, I've always done what I thought was good.

My friends and family all live with you
I want to be with them, my time is long over due.
What purpose does this frail old man have here?
Even my memory is getting sometimes unclear.

Linda Laybolt
Whispers From Heaven

Always, you have been a very good friend to me
Many times you shined your light so I could see.
You've given me strength so many times, to go on
When all hope seemed lost, and everything went wrong.

Comfort and compassion, I'll never forget
For all eternity, I'll be in your debt.
I'll always love you for all that you've done
I'll always be grateful for being your loved one!

But most of all Lord, I am so humble to you
For all the pain and suffering for me, that you went through!
I know there were many times you carried me along
And now wrapped in your arms is where I belong!

The Lord wrapped his arms around the old man
And said, like any other day, I have a great plan!
Close your eyes and rest my weary friend
We are on the last road, Heaven is just around the bend!

Today I Said Good-bye....

So you've lost a dear loved one, close to you
You're feeling sad and lost, and don't know what to do.
The tears fall and fall from your heart, without end
Just when you think they've stopped, they start all over again.

You wish you could turn back time, just one more day
For the things that were left unsaid, that you would like to say.
Just once more, you long to see that smiling face
Or feel the touch of that warm embrace.

You would love to look into those glowing eyes
Or hear that loving voice, instead of your lonely cries.
Please don't cry any more tears for me
Because where I'm at, I'm happy as can be.

Linda Laybolt
Whispers From Heaven

Today, I walked through Heavens Gates
I was so excited, I could hardly wait!
I was never alone, when I departed from you
My Guardian Angel was right beside me, always in full view.

Even though it seemed like I was sound asleep
I was standing beside you all, watching you quietly weep.
I placed my loving arms around each of you
Softly kissed you goodbye for now, but none of you knew.

My Angel told me, it was time to go Home, she led the way
I did not abandon you all, and forever go away!
So don't be sad and feel lost and blue
Because up here in Heaven, I can see all of you!

The day will come, when we will all be together
And live in God's Everlasting Love, forever and ever.
So next time, you think of me, think of all the love
That is waiting for you, up here in Heaven Above!

The Holy Bible

Although I may be plain outside on my cover
Once I am opened, there is so much in here for you to discover
I have many, many pages to be read
So many things written in here that I wanted to be said.

You may not quite understand exactly
What my words mean, all the time
But if you keep reading what I have written
You will find the meaning in between, the fine lines.

The important history in my book is all you need to know
It was written by many for thousands of years
Passed down from generation to generation
There's more in this book, than the outside appears.

Linda Laybolt
Whispers From Heaven

I hold all the answers that you search for
Everything including creation in this universe divine
There is absolutely nothing that I don't know about
Because everything around you is mine.

There is no better teacher than I, that exists
I can teach you what is right and what is wrong
All you have to do is keep reading my words
And you will see that in my family, you do belong.

You will learn about my only son, Jesus Christ
Who came to earth for not only you, but all mankind
His love for you is told in how he lived and died
No greater love for you than in him, you will ever find.

Go ahead, pick up my book and glance through it
For it was written for all to behold
All the books in it were written by my prophets
They wrote exactly what I wanted to be told.

There are only two words that appear on my cover
And that is Holy Bible, you see
I am the original author, I am your Most Holy Lord
I wrote this book out of love for you, for all eternity!

Take My Burdens

My heart is so full of sadness these days
The pain within just won't go away
No matter what I do, nothing seems right
Morning, noon and night.

Tears seem to want to forever flow
The heartache never wants to let go.
So much to ponder and think about
Makes me feel like, I am all worn out.

Linda Laybolt
Whispers From Heaven

The skies are not blue anymore, just dark and grey
Yet everyone thinks that I am ok.
Little do they know that my heart cries inside
The hurt and the tears stand side by side.

But I have decided that today is the day
I'm making a change as I don't want to stay this way.
I'm so grateful Lord that you are there
And that you really for me, do care.

So I am placing all my burdens in your loving hands
I know you are the one, who completely understands.
Today is the day Lord, I really need you
So I'm asking for your love to carry me through.

In the past to me, you've remained loyal and true
And that's why My Dear Lord, I want you to take all my burdens with you.

God Bless All Those

God bless all the little angels here
Always hold them close and near
Keep them all safe and warm
Especially when they shed a tear.

God bless all those in need
Even if they don't turn to you
You have so much comfort to give
Especially when they require help get through.

God bless all those who are in pain
From the cries within their heart
Show them all the compassion you have
Especially when their world seems to fall apart.

Whispers From Heaven

God bless all those who are ill
And do not wish to carry on
Give them strength and will to live
Especially when there is no one else to depend upon.

God bless all those who live in poverty
When everyday seems full of more sorrow
Let them know that you are there and care
Especially when all hope is lost of a brighter tomorrow.

God bless all those in war
Or live in conflict everyday
Show them that you a merciful God
Especially when you with you, there is a better way.

God bless all those who have disabilities
Of every possible kind
Let them feel your presence within
Especially when they long for peace of mind.

God bless all those who feel lost and alone
Let know you are close and near
Wrap your loving arms around them
Especially when they have something to fear.

God bless all those who live by your word
And put their love, faith and trust in you
Let them always carry your most divine love
Especially when their hearts are sincere, genuine and true.

The Lost Sheep

Only you can hear the silent cries
Of your children as they weep
A crying soul, in their heart lies
From your flock, they are your lost sheep.

Just wandering, existing from day to day
Living in darkness, forever they roam
Trapped in a place, where out of, they cannot stray
Always searching for that field, they call home.

Hurting one another, without blinking an eye
Yet in the silence, you can hear the soul cry
Just like the biblical times, many years ago
The ways of your children have hurt your heart so.

Someday out of the darkness, they will come
With that ray of light, the soul will push them through
Only cries of joy from the soul you will hear
For the pasture they longed for, is right here with you.

Most Faithful Lord

There are times Lord, I feel I have not done my best
Times, I feel I have let you down
Times that I may have turned my back on you
But you always stay near, forever turning me back around.

What have I done to deserve such worthiness from you
Guiding me to the right path for me to see
For you know, sometimes I do get weak and fall
Still you stand right here diligently, beside me.

Your love is like the waters in the river that endlessly flow
Or like the beautiful rainbow as it glows throughout the sky
I don't know what I would ever do without you
I'd be lost and lonely if you left and was not nearby.

Lord, we talk about us putting our faith in you
But it's you that so willingly puts your faith in all of us
Forever with us giving your unconditional love so freely
Making you the one that I truly love, honor, obey and trust.

Thank You

When I say, I need you
For sometimes, its hard to know what to do
You come be my ray of light
To do what is right.

When I feel lonely inside
From the world, I want to hide
You are the one, I can depend
To be my friend.

When everything seems to go wrong
Finding it hard to move on
You always find a way
To get me through the day.

When sad, my heart starts to ache
Feeling it is going to crumble and break
You come wipe the tears away
To help make it okay.

When I feel , I can no longer walk
For life seems like a stumbling block
You come lift me up, without delay
To carry me part of the way.

When life feels like a cold endless storm
For nothing will keep me warm
You come fill my heart with your love
It's you, My Dear Lord, I'm speaking of.

The Long Road

So many times Lord,you have lifted me up to carry me
For the road of life can be very winding and long
So many obstacles along the way
Always walking beside me, giving strength to move on.

Day after day, we travel together
Through the blistering sun and the pouring rain
Many road stones to stumble over, making me fall down
Constantly picking me up,forever taking away all of my pain.

Searching for what, I do not know
Following a different path, every now and then
Leading us to unknown places and sites,that we have never been
Sometimes, stopping for a short time,and then off we go again.

I am not sure how long this journey will take us
Many trials and tribulations, we will face along the way
I will not abandon you, as you would never leave me
Your timeless love, helps me get through each and every day.

My friend forever, with me you always will be
Walking beside me, together as we roam
Someday soon, this road, we will no longer walk
For at the end of it is our destination, our beautiful, heavenly home.

Let Me Live

Praise be to you, My Most Holy Lord
Let me live my life ,only by your accord.
Let me have compassion for those all around me
For love in my heart is all, I want them to see.

Linda Laybolt
Whispers From Heaven

Let me walk freely with a clear conscience in my mind
For in it , no wrong doings, I want for you to find.
Let my love radiate like no other
For your word is always to love one another.

Let my faith for you, come shining through
For there is only room for one God and that is you.
Let me put trust in you, Oh Mighty One
As my forefathers did, and Jesus, your only son.

Let me obey your commandments every day
As Moses did, showing us your righteous way.
Let me manifest your love with acts of kindness
For even a smile can bring happiness.

Let me give hope to those whose dreams have become fears
Showing tenderness while I help wipe away the tears.
Let me honor you with dignity and respect
For I know it's the least from me, you should expect.

But most of all Lord, let me carry your love in my heart always
So all can see in me, your infinite, most gracious, loving ways.

The Abandon Church

Out in the country on a lonely dirt road
Stands a House of God that looks to be falling down
The shingles are all weather stained
Brown grass filled with weeds grow upon the ground.

Out in the back of it, a black steel fence has faded
Most stones still stand in the cemetery here
Full of solitude, now long forgotten
Refusing to crumble from age to slowly disappear.

Linda Laybolt
Whispers From Heaven

Once where a gleaming white fence stood
Lurks broken wood waiting for its final fall
The wooden steps have also taken their toll with age
However, God's house still stands mighty and tall.

As you enter inside, the door opens with great ease
Carefully watch where you step, for you may fall through
No one has been in here for many a year's
Lonely and empty, God's house that once, so many came into.

As you look around, it's really small in here
Through the cobwebs on the windows, the light still shines bright
Although dust covers the pews, have a seat anyway
Look down, you'll find a book that's been long due out of sight.

As you gently open it, turn the fragile pages with tender care
For it's my Holy Scriptures, full of Hymns and Prayers
Now stand up, reverently read some prayers to me
Then lift up your voice singing hymns, throughout the air.

And when it's time for you to leave, don't feel sad inside
I am happy you came to visit me for a while
Just remember, my door is never shut, forever it remains open
For today, my child, you entered my house and it made me smile.

Jesus, My Ever-Loving Saviour

It brings a lump to my throat and a tear forms in my eye
When I hear about all the suffering and pain that you went through
I know it happened many years ago, well before my time
But thoughts of any harm to God's only son, breaks my heart in two.

I know you came here willingly, sent by your loving Father
Who reigns in heaven above
But how they mistreated, abused, and persecuted you
Is not what I call brotherly love.

Whispers From Heaven

How all of heaven must have wept and cried
While upon that cross, you did lay
Asking only forgiveness for what they had done
You paid the ultimate price for our sins that day.

You are The Messiah, Jesus, My Ever-Loving Saviour
Son of God, King of Kings, forever and thereof
Knowing all things, what was to be
Still, you came for us and died with your heart so full of love.

Forever Loving You, My Lord

Each and every morning, at the start of a new day
A soft whisper of I Love You Lord can be heard
Meek and humble, I stand before you
Trying to live and to abide by your holy word.

You have given me so much to be grateful for
I honestly don't know where to begin
So many times my soul has been given comfort
Deep love and compassion fill my heart from within.

Your unconditional love is divine and timeless
Like the graceful waters that gush against the shore
Forever recurring, continuous and infinite
Patiently flowing, now and forevermore.

Your eminent patience, compassion, and kindness
Never ceases to amaze me
Helpful, provider, giver and forgiver
Are very few words to describe thee.

You are a calm, merciful, jealous and most powerful God
Decisive ,trustworthy and fulfilling
The Creator of all the heavens and earth
I pledge my love for you, very most willing.

Almighty ,Supreme, Absolute, the Alpha and the Omega
For all time, from the beginning till the end
Thankfully and righteously, I give praise to you, Blessed be Thy Holy Name
For you are my loving Father and Most Gracious Lord, whom upon, I can always depend.

My Lord, My Friend

Almighty Lord, Creator of all things, I adore you
I put no other God before you
You are my shining light of each passing day
For without you, there is no other way.

You know everything there is to know about me
No secrets from you ever, could there possibly be
You are my closest friend so I never feel lonely
For you are my God, my one and only.

You are the foundation of life, that I can lean on
You hold the loving shoulder that I can laugh or cry upon
You walk beside me every step of the way
Throughout the passing of each and every day.

When in despair, and it seems like no one understands
I place my troubles, into your loving hands
When the road gets weary and dark, making it unable to see
You lift me up into your arms and gently carry me.

Although you reign in heaven above
You are the one that fills my heart with love
And because of this, I never will stray
So with you My Lord, my Friend, forever I will stay.

I Love You Lord

I love you Lord and thank you, for the new day that is about to begin
The darkness of night is fading, dawn slowly arises before me
Birds singing, dew drops everywhere, the freshness of the air
I am so grateful you created morning for us to enjoy and see.

I love you Lord for all beauty of nature, that you so carefully placed here for us
From your glorious high mountains to scenic oceans, rivers and lakes
By day, sometimes a perfect blue sky; by night, stars twinkling ever so bright
The beauty of your colorful rainbow or that of the delicate, elegant snowflakes.

I love you Lord for all the different species of animals, birds, fish and bugs
While some are annoying, I know you placed them here with love
The graceful wings of a bird as it flies, or the sweet sounds it sings
Could only sent by you, My Lord, who reigns in heaven above.

I love you Lord for the earthly family that you have given me
I thank you for all the people and friends I have met throughout my days
I know my life is just as you planned
With tears of hardship and sorrow, laughter and joy, could it be any other way.

I love you Lord, I want to do what is right
To be a kind, forgiving, loving person to all around me
To help and give comfort, to those around me in need
Even if, all it takes is a kind word or smile, I hope you agree.

I love you Lord, I know that each road you lead me to
Sometimes may be bumpy along the way
But you walk with me every step that I take
I know you never will leave, with me always you will stay.

Linda Laybolt
Whispers From Heaven

I love you Lord with all my heart and soul
I know I don't tell you often enough, that's why I wrote this poem for you
You are my God, Creator and Most Holy Father
That's why I am sending it to you with love, for I know in my heart that you love me too.

Have Faith in Me, Your Lord

Just because you do not see me, does not mean I am not here
I am always with you, my child, and my love for you will never disappear.
It's funny the way the world is today, the things people say and do
Because my words written down so many years ago were for you and are so very true.

You say creation of the earth, once started with the sun
So tell me now, where exactly did the sun come from?
The scientists say that man is traced back in time as a descendent of the ape
So if so-called evolution exists, why have you not evolved as a descendent from man's shape?

You send your man-made rockets up in the sky, ever searching for extra-terrestial life
So why do you say, I don't exist but in the end want to come to me in the afterlife?
You claim it's a thing called progress,every country wants to rule the earth and be number one
So if this is so, why from heaven, did I send you the King of Kings ,Jesus, my one and only son?

You let the children of the earth go hungry, when there's more than enough for all
So please explain to me, why I gave you plenty to survive, is greed your biggest downfall?

Linda Laybolt
Whispers From Heaven

When you see things that you think may be a potential threat, you jump right in and go to war
So where is the love and peace I placed in your heart for all mankind, I stand for?

You take my name in vain, then commit wrong-doing on others
Tell me why then, I call you my children and proclaim that you are all sisters and brothers?
You seemed to have forgotten that I consider Sunday, the seventh day, a day of rest
So why did I make it my day of worship, was that such a huge request?

You continually break all my commandments that was set forth for you and think that it's o.k.
Whatever happened to honoring, loving, trusting me, and let's not forget obey?
You look up to the sky and complain you need to see a miracle, just like your forefathers before
Why not take a look around, they happen everyday, but yet you ask for more?

With all this being said and done, why is it so hard to put some Faith into me?
Creator of all things, heaven and earth are full of my glory
I am the Alpha and the Omega,"who is, and who was, and who is to come,the Almighty"
I am the Lord, Your Loving God!

Trapped Deep Within

The young man was approximately 29 years old
He made funny noises, with grunts here and there
He could not keep still, fumbling around
A feeling of sadness floated through the air!

We see this picture quite often, everywhere we go
People with disabilities, who we think cannot understand
Some are locked away forever while others are not
Every parents nightmare, completely unplanned!

Some parents keep their children with them
Raise them up to adulthood, as best they can
Others cannot cope and send their child away
This has been happening for years, since the world began!

Even if they are kept at home to be raised
The parents days are tiring and endless, full of lost hope
The stress can be over-powering at times
Yet, they always succumb to love and find a way to cope!

Imagine what it is like for the person with the disability
Feeling trapped, deep within, a lost soul
Shunned and ignored by our so-called society
Trying to reach out, seldom ever to feel consoled!

When I look into the eyes of one these people
I see the complete look of innocence, from within
I believe that they are exactly as God intended
Sent to earth from Heaven, living without sin!

Could they possibly be one of God's many messengers?
Or possibly an angel in disguise sent from above?
To me, they are the only humans that exist on earth, without sin
The innocent smile they carry, and the eyes say it all, LOVE!

The Unicorns

The two looked at each other with their heads held high in the air
Throughout the forest, their beauty and elegance was felt everywhere!
All the animals respected them, they were different than all the rest
Many referred to them as the ones, that God created best!

The unicorn legend has been around for years so it is said
But does anyone know how this fantasy became so wide spread?
It's funny, it is written in the Bible about the unicorn
Yet, one the great mysteries, is how much they were adorn!

Yet, we have such a vivid description of what they looked like back then
Passed down from generation to generation, time and time again!
It is not known neither about how they are no longer in our sight
But curiosity makes me think, there is more to it, something is just not right!

So I am going to give my thoughts on this, I know there is a big chance that I am wrong
I will try to make it short, but this poem could end up very long!
When God created all animals, he wanted one that held beauty like no other
So he only made two unicorns, so they would always love one another!

He made them white because white in his eyes, represents only the pure
A beautiful single horn in the centre of their head, which was unusual, for sure!

Linda Laybolt
Whispers From Heaven

He gave them great strength as that of an oxen, speed of a black panther
And he gave them wisdom to understand, beyond any other!

Oh the mighty, beautiful unicorn, where have you gone?
You are no longer here, but I think that you do live on!
Because if you all remember the story, about how it went
Everyone was trying to capture the unicorns,which caused them great dissent!

I think that God decided one day, with Him, they should be
So he just took them from the earth, to Heaven to run free!
But in my mind, I think the day will come, when all will see them in good turn
In all Mighty and Glory, with Our Lord Jesus, when he returns!

Mankind Needs To Change

No matter what explanation they come up with
Creation by God, is definitely not a myth!
The scientists think they have it all solved
Concerning evolution, how man evolved!

They say that long time ago, we were an ape
And through time, we changed our shape!
What an insult to the Lord and to all of us
Man's high-technology, so called progress!

Funny, isn't it, they can put a man on the moon
But yet, they can't stop the winds of a typhoon!
They say they have all the answers
But then again,no known cure for cancer!

They secretly build their nuclear bombs, piece by piece
Then, they all say, we want world peace!
Little children die from hunger and poverty everyday
Yet countries still declare, help is somewhere on the way!

Linda Laybolt
Whispers From Heaven

All the weather pattern changes, is from global warming
Have you heard the earth is continually transforming?
The earthquakes, the tidal waves, the mighty storms
Better take cover, it's not our fault, the governments warn!

As soon as one new disease in under control
Another one is surfacing, all ready to roll!
Money given without hesitation in research, for our benefit
How do we benefit from a nuclear bomb, I just don't get it!

Oh mankind sure has developed and evolved over time
More like they have gotten deeper into world crime!
Wars upon wars, never cease but continue to arise
Is it just me, can no one hear the little childrens cries?

It's just not all the things that I have talked about
Somewhere along the line, man's conscience faded out!
Lashing out at each other, sisters and brothers
Never thinking about the hurt, they cause one another!

There is so much wrong-doing and hatred that exists today
Our world is not happy but full of dismay!
Fears of tomorrow, fears of the unknown
Fears of what will happen next, has been planted and sewn!

Who were these people that brought to us, so much shame
Was it the teacher or the scientist, who is the blame?
Or did we bring it upon ourselves, possibly for gain
Huh! I think it's all wrong and so inhumane!

I am sorry I drifted away from my poem
But sometimes, my mind just wants to roam and roam!
So I am going to start this all over for you
I hope I haven't made you feeling sad and blue!

Linda Laybolt
Whispers From Heaven

Our Loving Lord who lives in Heaven above
Created the earth for us, out of love!
He gave us everything that we needed to live
There was nothing needed for us to survive!

Enough of everything was here for all to get by
It must sadden Our Lord, to hear his children cry!
His beautiful Earth, now full of sorrow and despair
Mainly because mankind was so greedy, not willing to share!

All the Lord ever wanted for us was Peace, Joy and Love
Just as it is, in His Heaven above!
We cannot blame Our Lord, for the mess that we're in
What we all need to do, is make changes to our hearts, from deep within!

The Trumpet

What is that noise, coming from the sky?
Sounds like a loud horn, coming from way up high.
Could it be one of God's angels sending out a warning sign?
That something miraculous is about to take place and truly divine!

In recent years, these sounds have emerged from nowhere
Scientists have no answers, yet it mysteriously flows through the air.
It can be heard in every corner of the world, so it seems
Appearing like a thief in the night, a horn it is, by all means!

I've heard it said that Jesus will come like a thief in the night
Is this horn a warning to all, that He will soon be in sight?
Is mankind going to keep ignoring the fact, that Our Lord Jesus
Will soon be coming back to earth, just as He has promised us?

Yes, a divine miracle is going to take place soon one day
After hearing that horn, it could be today!
Your children are waiting with anticipation for you
Our Saviour, Our King, Our Lord Jesus, "We love you!"

Angels we hear the sound of the horn and its loud ring
Hallelujah! Hallelujah! To Our Mighty King!

And Jesus Ascended Into Heaven...

When the Cross of Glory rises for all to see
All Gods Children will bow in Humility
For Jesus will Reign of All The Heavens and the Earth
And life for His Followers will be given "A New Birth."

All the pain and suffering, He suffered on the Cross
Will never again be referred to as the worlds loss
The Second Coming will finally have arrived
Those who follow Him, will be grateful to be alive.

For without warning, out of the Heavens, Jesus will come
A great day it will be, but only for some.
Imagine the shock may years ago when Jesus rose from the dead
Fear filled most people then, so it is said!

Just imagine what it is going to be like for us who believe
But for the non-believers, it will be hard to perceive.
How sad it must have been after all the good deeds he done
To be abandoned by his own followers, Gods Beloved and Only Son.

But when He returned from Hades, before ascending into Heaven
His Disciples carried on His works, they knew they were forgiven!
Happiness fills my soul knowing that Jesus will return soon someday
Perhaps maybe it could even be this Blessed Easter Sunday!

God The Almighty Spoke To His People...

Cracks of thunder and lightning surrounded the earth
The Lord in Heaven had decided, it's time for a spiritual rebirth!
The sky opened up and a loud voice could be heard
I have something to say, so carefully listen to me Word for Word!

Do not be afraid, all ears and eyes have been opened
All barriers of languages has been broken!
Not one person on earth will not be able to understand
For what I have to say, is coming to you firsthand!

Look up towards the sky, God announced in a Mighty voice
I am taking back what is mine, you give me no choice!
I created all the Heavens and Earth, out of Love
I see it slowly is being destroyed, from Heaven Above!

Linda Laybolt
Whispers From Heaven

I am the Alpha and Omega, what was, is and yet to come
I am God the Creator, from where all living things has come from!
Some of you think I do not exist, just because you cannot see me
But I am here to tell you, with you I always have been and always will be!

I have watched in silence, hoping you would change your ways
You say a miracle from God, we need these days!
I give you miracles all the time, yet still, you do not believe
You are just not paying attention, how my heart grieves!

I could go on for years naming miracles one by one
But I am only going to mention my greatest miracle and that was My Son!
I sent Him to you, out of love for you on a cross, he died
Eternal life can be yours, yet some of you hast cast Him aside!

Soon, My Son Jesus and His Army, out of the Heavens will descend
To gather the Tribes of Israel, my people, to Heaven they will ascend!
There will be nothing left here on Earth to protect any of you
There will be no place to run and hide from my wrath, this is true!

Loud cracks of thunder roared across the Earth as The Lord continues to speaks again
Children of the Earth, You are mine and Forever, I will reign!
I created you all from the love from my heart, and I still love you
Prepare for the Second Coming, for the Earth will be made anew!

With these final words, the skies turned blue, rays of light came shining through
Was The Lord in Heaven giving His people one more final chance, on what they should do?
This was truly an eye-opener for those who did not believe
The Lord Almighty had spoken, for all to hear and perceive!

Well, as you all know, this never happened, but I wish it would
Then the Lords Word by all, would be understood!
What is it going to take for a spiritual awakening today?
For all God's Children to come Home to His Love, Forever, to stay!

Down In The Valley, Gods Love Reigns

Down in the valley, where the sun shines
Gods love reigns, just look at the signs
Little birds fly to and fro to their young
With new lullabies, waiting to be sung.

Insects gather food for the day
Mice run and play amongst the hay
The rooster lets out his cock a doddle do
Saying Good Morning All, Good Morning to you!

The farmer rises before dawn
He's busy with a barn to build upon
Even the dog and cat are on the go
Sometimes, however taking life slow.

Down by the old creek, water slowly gushes by
While an eagle flies through the open sky
Life is busy down here you know
Gods love reigns, everywhere you go.

Cows graze in the dark green pastures
Horses play to see who runs faster
Little lambs stick close to their mothers
Little goats try to jump rocks to be with others.

Even the wildlife is busy on the go
The mother fox searches for food for her young to grow
The deer hide deep in solitude in the woods
Along with the moose and young in the backwoods.

Down here in the valley, Gods love reigns
Everyone goes about their day, nobody complains
And at the end of each and everyday
All are thankful to God for sending His Love their way!

God Hears And Sees

God listens to all those who pray
He hears every word that you say.
Never give up on your hopes & dreams

Linda Laybolt
Whispers From Heaven

God has a plan especially for you, by all means.

God is everywhere, miracles happen in our times
Not just now & then, but everyday there are signs.
Take a look around you, they are in full view
Perhaps, one day a miracle will shine down on you.

When you pray, be thankful for each & every day
Rejoice & give Praise for the Blessings, that come your way.
Glance around at your life, things aren't really that bad
Think positive and be happy, not sad!

If you are in a situation, that does not agree with you
Remember God is always there, to see you through.
You are there for a reason, you have a path destined to walk along
God knows what He is doing, God is never wrong!

So next time you decide to have a chat with God, The Almighty
Remember, He is everywhere; there is nothing He does not see.
Your Father keeps a close watch on you, from Heaven Above
And shines a light on you, full of eternal Love!

Time For Truth!

The dawn has not yet broken, darkness still lingers outside
Just wondering to myself, how many will let Jesus be their guide
Today, how many will worship The King of Kings with Praise and Glory
How many will deny Him, as if He is a made up story?

How many out their will blame God because their life is going wrong?
How many will scorn God and say this is your fault, all day long?
How many will have the nerve to say, how could you do this to me?
How could you let an innocent child suffer and die, Your the Great Almighty?

How many will blame God The Father for all the wars going on?
How many turn away from God to other man-made idols to depend upon?
How many will look to the sky and yell, why me Lord?
What did I do to deserve this? Have I not lived by your accord?

How many will blame God for a loved one being molested, harmed or killed?
How many will say "There is no God" and let their hearts with hate be filled!
How many will decide to take their own life today, thinking no one cares?
How many will say, there has to be a better life than this out there?

How many chidren will be bullied at school today and not tell anyone?
How many women and children willl be abused, by a close loved one?
How many will point their finger at God, saying you are the blame?
You put me in this mess, now I live everyday in fear, pain and shame!

How many will keep turning their backs on God and blaming Him?
How many will keep denying Him and living in sin?
I think people should look differently as to where the blame goes
Because it is being directed wrongly, and the list just grows and grows!

It says that in the latter days, that mankind will turn their backs on God
That He will be denied and a false prophet will arise, full of fraud!
Take a look around, this has been happening now for many years
But hardly anyone realizes, he lives amongst us, feeding on our fears!

I hate to even say his name, as he is not worthy to be written about
Satan is turning Gods Children away from Him, beyond any doubt!
When God gets the blame for everything wrong in the world today
It should be Satan getting the scolding, he is the source of all evil, all the way!

Denying God The Father and His Son Our Lord Jesus is not for you
God is Love, God is not evil so why blame Him for things, He did not do?
Satan is sitting back having a great laugh, he has mankind thinking his way
But he can laugh all he wants, for he will get his due one of these days.

It's time to start to condemn Satan for what he has done
He may have most of the world fooled, but not Gods loved ones.
This is the biggest propaganda that Satan has ever pulled off in history
Its time to expose him fully and all that revolves around him in mystery!

Linda Laybolt
Whispers From Heaven

I have no fear of Satan for the Lord, My God walks with me
His rod and staff will protect me, He is The Great Almighty!
I love my Heavenly Father in Heaven, I love My Lord Jesus
It hurts me to see what Satan is doing to Our God and to us!

It's time to remember The Song Of Moses and Miram
And the love and faith, they held for Our God!

Who amongst the gods is like you Lord....Who is like you?
Majestic in Holiness
Awesome in Glory!
Working Wonders?
The Lord is My Strength and Song
And He has become My Salvation
He is My God and I will Praise Him!
My Fathers God and I will exalt Him!
The Lord is a Warrior;
And the Lord is His Name!
Sing Halleluijah To Your Majesty!

This poem was Inspired By God!

I Will Never Forget My People

As I gaze at the magnificent rainbow that stretches across the sky
I think of the covenant that God made to us from way up high.
It reminds me that Our Father in Heaven is never far away
And He has never forgotten us, to this very day.
Our Heavenly Father loved us so much, that He sent His Son
Jesus to walk amongst us, spreading His Fathers Love to everyone.
Healing the sick along the way, performing miracles every day
Restoring Faith and Love in Humanity, was The Lords Way.
Forever being ridiculed by some, even betrayed by His very own
Yet, He never forgot why He was here, the seeds of love were sown.
The Son Of God, The Lord Jesus walked the earth Full Of Love
Spreading His Fathers Word to mankind, from Heaven Above.
At the end of His journey, He gave His life for all of us
The Lord will never forget His people, and we will never forget you,
Our Saviour, Most Holy Lord Jesus!

High Up In The Heavens Above

High up in the Heavens Above
The angels worship you with Love
With praise and glory, they sing to you
Someday Lord, I know I will be there too!

In my heart, I know the day will come
When I will see your Mighty Kingdom
When I see the twelve Pearls of Gates
Inside I know, Divine Love Awaits!

When I see you standing there,
It will be difficult, not to shed a tear
As the light of your divine love surrounds me
It is then, finally my spirit will be set free!

When I see your glowing face
Arms held out for me to embrace
I will know I'm Home at last
What once was, is now the forgotten past!

When I see the scars you bare
I will know how much you really care
The pain and suffering you went through
Just to bring me Home, to be with you!

I will bow down on my knees
And thank you Lord, for saving me
All praise and glory, I will give to you
Tears will fall, my heart in full view!

I will thank you, for all the times
You carried me, your light on me always did shine
Loving me throughout my earthly stay
Giving me the gift of eternal life today!

Linda Laybolt
Whispers From Heaven

High up in the Heavens Above
The angels worship you with Love
With praise and glory, they sing to you
Someday Lord, I know I will be there too!

Love And Faith

I speak of Love
Sent from Above!
I write of Jesus
Who was sent to us!
By Love
From His Father Above!

In The Beginning, I spoke of Love
Love is where it all began, in Heaven Above!
I am Alpha and Omega, the Beginning and the End
Only through My Son, can all Mankind transcend!
In order to do that, you must have Love in your heart
Otherwise, how will I be able to tell my children apart?
Some believe that Faith is the only way
To receive my Blessings, you have to pray!
This is partially true but there is more to this
To live with Me and My Son Jesus, in Eternal Bliss!
Which brings me back to Love, the Love I have for you
Spoken and written of, by my many messengers, for you to pursue!
In order to have Faith, you must have Love for My Son and Me
Like the Love I have for you, for all Mankind to see!
I am the One who created you out of Love, from the ground
Man did not create me, it's the other way around!
My Son willingly gave His life for you on a wooden cross, He Died
All out of Love for you, and yet some still cast Him Aside!
So Love comes above all, Love for Jesus, My Beloved Son
He is the Way, He is the Light of the World, He Is The One!
When you have Love, you have true Faith in God Above
When you have Faith, You will always have God's Divine Love!

John 3:16
For God so loved the world, that he gave his only begotten Son, that whosoever believeth in him should not perish, but have everlasting life.

The Waves Of Life

In solitude, I watch the darkness of night
As it slowly disappears, fading away
Warmth from the rays of light gently appear
Bringing along the start of a new day!

As I make my way down to the shore
The smell of the ocean fills the air
Sea gulls call to each other off in the distant
The sounds of the waves, can be heard everywhere!

My feet are warm from the soft pebbles of sand
The sun now is shining brightly, in the blue sky
No clouds can be seen today, as I glance up
Out in the ocean, a small boat passes by!

Timeless and free are the waves
Rushing to the shore
With grace and splendor, the waves triumph
As they take the floor!

Surging back and forth
With the passing of the tide
Infinitely, dancing and singing
Always, side by side!

As they surge against the shore
Their journey has come to an end, at last
What was once a beautiful wave
Is now a manifestation of the past!

Linda Laybolt
Whispers From Heaven

As I watch the waves, ceasing to exist
I realize that, for them a new life is about to begin
For back to the mighty ocean, they will return
Transforming into a new wave, to come back in!

I contemplate to myself, life is a lot like this
At the end of our journey, life does not cease
Our body is just a shell, our soul deep inside lives forever
The new life that we have waited, is about to be released!

As the waves, disintegrate back to its home, the ocean
We also return back Home to Our Lord in Heaven
A new life begins for the waves, once again
A new life, full of bliss and peace, unto us is given!

The Promise

I am here at your side
My Dear Loving Friend
And here I will stay
Until the very end!
I feel the sadness in your heart
I can see the tears in your eyes
I promise not to let go of your hand
As you say, your final good-byes!
All the family is here with you
Gathered quietly around your bed
All preparations have been made for you
The final prayers have all been said!
You have lived your life
With love in your heart
Placing it in others, all around you
A gift given, that will never depart!
Your life was full of hardships
With happy times along the way
Many times you came to me for help

Knowing, I'd never turn you away!
As you take, your final breaths of life
And depart from your loved ones here
Do not feel sad or lonesome
For those feelings, will soon disappear!
As I said before. My Dear Friend
I promise not to let go, of your loving hand
All tears have been wiped away, your face now glows
As we enter the Gates Of Home, "My Father's Promised Land!"

God's Little Angels

Sometimes God sends His little angels to earth on loan
Borrowed angels that will be called back Home!
Some are here for only a very short while, others longer
They bring love in our life, which eventually makes us stronger!
We search for answers as to why this was to be
Through heartbreak and tears, most times, it is difficult to see!
That this little bundle of joy, that was given in love
Was an angel on loan sent by God, in Heaven above!
Sometimes, we turn our back on God, blaming Him for this
Failing to remember, that this little angel is His!
They may be here on earth with you for a very long time
And their light of love, on you will shine!
He has sent this little angel to you for reasons, yet unknown
And now has left you feeling heart-broken, lost and alone!
Think of it as a great blessing, which has been bestowed upon you
Not as a sadness of the past, trying not to look back to
High up in the Heavens, a special angel watches over you
Sending you their love, in everything you do
God loved you so much, that he sent His Special Angel to you
But only on loan, to bring love to you!

I Believe In The Power Of Love

Carry my love in your heart, where ever you go
As the days and years pass by you, feel it grow and grow
Never feel alone or afraid, for I am with you
Watching over you, always in full view!

There will be many times that you stray away from me
None of My Children are perfect, all carry sin, you see
But whatever path or road, you choose to wander
Your free will decides the outcome, perhaps making you stronger.

You may think that I cannot see you at all times
Don't forget I Am God; All things are possible, not just sometimes.
I hear every word that is said, every thought that runs in your mind
Every wrong thing and every act you do that is kind.

My Love will always be with you, You are My Children, My Own
Your Life here is just a stepping stone, till you come Home
And when you return, I will be waiting for you with arms open wide
And we will walk through Heavens Gates, side by side!

Time To Remember

I will follow you anywhere you want me to
You are my Lord Jesus who died for me, Thank You!
You paid the debt for my sins, something I am so grateful for
I owe my life to you and so much more!
You came to earth on your own free will for all of mankind
You taught us all about love, no greater love than yours, I'll ever find.
Thousands of years have passed since you lived here on earth amongst us
But I will never forget you, My Dear Saviour, My Precious Lord Jesus!
The pain and suffering that you endured just to set my sins free
Forever, I will Praise you My Lord Jesus in the highest degree!
It's almost that time of the year again, to remember all you have done
Most Holy Precious Lord, God's Chosen Beloved Son!
Lord of Lords, King of Kings; Forever shall you reign
The Heavens and Earth and all of your great domain!
Forever, your Angels and Children will sing unto you for All Eternity
Halleluijah! To Our Lord Jesus....What Was, Is and Yet To Be!

Walking Beside Me

The Lord is my one true God, there is no other.
He walks with me each step that I take, one after another.
Even in my darkest hours, he makes his presence known
With him beside me, I never feel alone.

He is always there when I need him the most
Many times he holds next to him, nice and close.
Even when things don't seem right but unclear
He shines his light, letting me know he is near.

He shows me compassion, when everything goes wrong
His mighty strength is what keeps me moving along.
Even when everything is going right, he is there
He gives his divine love to me, for he truly does care.

He is with me whatever path I chose to walk upon
Sometimes it may not be straight but narrow and long
Even if it is not the path that I should be on
He walks with me through it, as I continue along.

No matter what I do or where I go to
My heart tells me, God is with you
I am never alone anywhere
Because my Lord is with me, always there.

WITH HIM, I SHALL NOT WANT

The Lord is my shepherd, I shall not want
The Lord is my lovingly one true god, no other shall I want.
The Lord lovingly is always in my heart
Without him, it would be torn apart.

With him, I shall not want!
The Lord lovingly shows me his compassion and kindness
He fills my heart with happiness.

Linda Laybolt
Whispers From Heaven

With him, I shall not want!
The Lord lovingly walks beside me every day
Every step, I take along the way.

With him, I shall not want!
The Lord lovingly guides and leads me
Teaching me his righteous ways for all to see.

With him, I shall not want!
The Lord lovingly feeds my soul with his Holy Scriptures to read
Making life so much easier to proceed.

With him, I shall not want!
The Lord lovingly teaches me what is right and what is wrong
He give me strength which makes my love for him, forever growing strong.

With him, I shall not want!
The Lord lovingly uses his arms to carry me when I feel, I cannot walk
For he is my Shepherd and I am one of his mighty flock.

With him, I shall not want!
The Lord loving with his hands will take all my burdens away
All I have to do is humbly ask and pray.

With him, I shall not want!
The Lord lovingly forgives me of all my sins
He fills me with peace and contentment, deep within.

With him, I shall not want!
The Lord lovingly reigns in heaven above
Forever sending us all, his unconditional love.
With him, there is nothing in this world that I ever want!
THE LORD IS MY SHEPHERD, I SHALL NOT WANT!

The Child In Me

The child in me wants to run and play in the sun
Chase after butterflies and frogs, through the meadows
Stumble and fall in the water, getting wet from head to toe
Running free with the wind, with no cares or sorrows!

The child in me wants to play in a big make believe fort
Nestled amongst the trees, with many rooms to play in
Prepare a huge dinner for my many guests and friends
One thing about here, there is no such thing as sin!

The child in me wants to run through the open fields
Stop and look in amazement at all the blooming flowers
Stand out in the pouring rain, laughing as I get soaked
No attention is given to seconds, minutes, or hours!

The child in me wants to go fishing in an old pond
With a pole made from a branch off a tree
Then, when I get bored, jump in for a swim
Having no worries or cares, just a spirit that is free!

The child in me would love to return to that old one room school
Where every day, I walked many miles to get to
Eating bread and molasses for lunch while playing with my friends
Does not sound like much, but we had lots to do!

The child in me misses the old church, we all attended on Sunday
It was the main gathering place for all who lived here
When the service was over, all gathered outside to talk
Children were always, smiling and laughing, no burdens to bare!

The child in me wishes things could be like back then
No questions were ever asked, you believed all that was said
Young and innocent, you had no reason not to believe in God
Where everynight, prayers were said to Him, before you went to bed!

The child in me can still go out and lay on the grass
Look up at the sky and watch the clouds, as they go by
Or sit back in amazement with wonder and awe
At the site of a rainbow, as it stretches across the sky!

As old as I am, the child in has never disappeared as many others
It will always be here to stay, even if only in my heart
But I will always be a child in my Lord's eyes, His Child
The child in me, from Him will never cease to depart!

It's Never Too Late

The sweet fragrances of summer fill the air
As flowers and trees bloom everywhere.
Birds are busy singing in the trees
Branches dance to the soft gentle breeze.
It seems as though a rebirth has begun
As nature and wildlife enjoy the summer sun.
As I sit here quietly looking around
I see so much beauty, to be found.
They say beauty is in the eye of the beholder
Never really appreciating it, until you are much older.
Now you have the time to stop and look
Or sit down and quietly read a book.
Whereas, before you were always on the go
Rushing through each day, following the flow.
Now is the time, you can reflect back
And question whether your life was really on track.
Now, you wonder about all the "if only"
And you question why, you feel so lonely!
There is something missing, it plays on your mind
You often wonder, what did I leave behind!
These days of worry can be gone today
Because Jesus is never far away!
Open your heart and let Him come in
A new life is waiting for you to begin!

No more worrying or feeling lonely
No more contemplating on the "if only"
Unconditional love and comfort await for you
Only you have the answer, as what to do!
Jesus said " I Am The Light"
So He is always, within your sight!

Children Of God

Everywhere I look, I see beauty surrounding me
In the childrens eyes, I see a young spirit, happy and free!
Solely dependent, too young, the ways of life to understand
Needing someone to walk through life, someone to hold their hand!
They are exploring constantly, learning about everything
They need someone that is loving, to take them under their wing!
Feeling loved and wanted, isn't that what it's all about?
Being able to give love back in return, not feeling left out!
Young and innocent, full of unconditional love
Precious are God's children, sent from Heaven above!
We are all children in God's eyes, whether young or old
Eternal Love is their waiting for all to Behold!

Matthew 19:14
But Jesus said Suffer little children, and forbid them not, to come unto me, for of such is the kingdom of heaven

Linda Laybolt
Whispers From Heaven

A Heart Without Love

No one seems to be content
Wondering around, full of torment!
Souls seem lost, all alone
Cast aside from life, like a stone!
No one comes to their rescue
Something they've grown accustomed to!
Some may have wealth, while others are poor
But all have hearts, that are tore!
Taking each day, one step at a time
Like a huge mountain, thats hard to climb!
Turning around, every now and then
Glancing at the past, remembering when!
Wondering if they will make it through today
When all hope seems lost, dark and grey!
Tomorrow is another day, not even thought of
The sadness and sorrow of a heart, without love!
But these days do not have to be at all
Love is always there at beckon and call!
No one ever has to feel lost and all alone
Or ever feel like, they have a heart of stone!
Love is waiting out there for all to receive
You just have to open your heart and believe!
Jesus is waiting with open arms for you
No more being alone, He will see you through!
The Lord's Love is for All Eternity!
Jesus said, Come to me!

The Path

I climbed a path with a never-ending hill that was way too long
Everything imaginary possible, seemed to go wrong!
I asked myself many times, when will this end?
Will there ever be peace and contentment in my soul again?

Whispers From Heaven

Each step I took along the way, there was something there to hinder me
I asked myself, Why me? How can this possibly be?
Bad luck is following me every move that I make
I really don't know how much more of this I can take!

Then I got to thinking, what have I really got to complain about?
The word nothing kept running through my mind, without any doubt!
The hill that I had just climbed was indeed way to long
But through it all, you were there with me, pushing me along!

So I had a little bit of bad luck, nothing seemed to go right
But you never left my side, or stopped shining your guiding light!
When I needed comfort and a shoulder to lean on
You surrounded me with love, till the last tear was gone!

Every path of life I take, leads me a different place
But also every path I take, you are near for me to embrace!
The path is only long and lonely, if you walk alone
But with you beside me, I can get over any rock or stone!

Thank you so much Lord for being here for me today and everyday
Always stay and walk with me each path I take, the whole way!
When we reach the path that is so full of light and love
Then, I will be on my way home with you to Heaven above!

The Book Of Love

The soft summer breeze gently flows from the trees
The fresh scent of flowers calms the mind with such ease!
Little birds songs can be heard throughout the air
The beauty of a summer evening, nothing else can compare!

Here she'd sit on her wooden veranda, in an old rocking chair
Years of wisdom prevailed upon her face, as did her grey hair!
Rocking back and forth, swaying as in in steady motion
Reading her precious book of love, with so much devotion!

Linda Laybolt
Whispers From Heaven

Now and again, she'd stop and pause, to have a glance around
And sit very quietly, without making a sound!
Many times I had asked her, What are you thinking of?
Always she replied, My Book Of Love!

Then she would rock and read till it was bedtime
And into the house, up the old wooden stairs, she would climb!
Every single night of life, before getting into bed
She got down on her knees, and a prayer to God was said!

She would thank him for giving her this day of life today
She would ask him to watch over her, as she slept the night away!
She would ask for blessings one by one, for each family member
And then she would add, your Book of Love, I will always remember!

I can remember standing outside her room at night
Listening to her pray when I was a kid, peeping out of her sight!
I remember I could understand her prayers
But the part about the Book Of Love, now that was a different affair!

Many years have come and gone, since way back then
I often reminisce about when I was a kid, time and time again!
I often think of my dear old Grandma sitting in her rocking chair
I often think of her Book Of Love and her sweet bedtime prayer!

Nowadays, the little old lady who was once called Grandma is me
I, too, sit in my rocking chair with my book, it is the place to be!
It took me years to comprehend why Grandma always called it the Book Of Love
But now, I know why for it was written by God Himself from Heaven above!

ALPHA AND OMEGA

On an old wooden cross, My Lord Jesus, My Saviour died
Three wooden crosses sat on Calvary Hill, side by side!
Not one of His followers spoke up, on His behalf for Him
The Son Of God, Emmanuel, who was born in Bethlehem!

My God, My God, Why hast thou forsaken me?, he cried out loud
Before he took His final breath, all heard Him that was in the crowd!
It saddens my heart, when I think of all the pain Jesus went through
Along with the betrayal of His followers, remaining with Him, stood only a few!

Two thousand years ago, the Son Of God walked amongst us
Most knew or had heard, the name of the Messiah was Jesus!
He went about the land with many followers, teaching His Father's Word
To the rich, the poor, the Gentiles and the Jews, who had not heard!

Many Words of Wisdom were spoken, along with many Words about Love
Love for one another, Love for God the Father, in Heaven above!
Jesus taught the Laws of His Father, the way he wanted us to live
God The Father wanted only the best for us, He wanted us to thrive!

While here on Earth, Jesus healed many people time after time
Many roads he had to walk, many mountains he had to climb!
Many miracles he performed, only the Son Of God could do
He never once complained about His Work, His loyalty remained true!

So why did so many people forsake Him, in His hour of need
Why did no one speak up and plead His case and intercede?
All of His followers supposedly loved and adored Him, so it is said
But when push came to shove, most became afraid, hid and fled!

Linda Laybolt
Whispers From Heaven

Three days after Jesus died on the cross, He arose from the dead
The news about the Messiah coming back to life, was widespread!
Even at first, many were in shock and disbelief, even His own mother
All who had heard of Him being alive, came to witness, one after another!

But Jesus was only to be seen, for a short while before ascending into Heaven
All scars from the crucifixion had vanished, as all sins of mankind forgiven!
Jesus had suffered and died for us, Lest We Never Forget
Eternal life is ours Forever To Behold, Our Lord Jesus pardoned us and paid the debt!

Alpha And Omega

You are Alpha and Omega
We worship you, Our Lord
You are worthy to be praised.
We give you all glory
We worship you, Our Lord
You are worthy to be praised.
You are the beginning of everything
Lord of Lords, King of Kings
You are worthy to be praised.
You are Our Lord and Saviour, too
We love you, through and through
You are worthy to be praised.

Be With Me Lord

Give me strength Lord to get through this day
I need you more than ever today
Give me your Wisdom Lord for you have so much to share
Guide me through this path that leads to who knows where.
Give me Courage to face the unknown

Linda Laybolt
Whispers From Heaven

Don't abandon me and leave me on my own
Be my Protector Lord, today of all days
Let me seek Refuge in you while giving you Praise.
Walk beside me Lord, on this and everyday
Lead me to the Path of Righteousness, this I humbly pray.
Let your Divine Light shine on me today
Let your ever-lasting Love surround me in every way.
Give me Hope Lord, when all else fails
Give me Peace of Mind, as your love prevails
Bless me O Lord, My Father in Heaven
Let all my earthly sins be forever Forgiven.
Walk with me Lord through the valley of death, if that be today
Let your rod and staff Comfort me, all the way
Then take me Home Lord ,to be with you
For you are my Father and I dearly love you!

If I Were Gods Helper

If I were Gods Helper here on earth
I'd change one thing for better with birth
Instead of having men as the Rulers....(except for God that is)
I'd have woman running everything, teaching the Schoolers...(the men)

First thing I would do is end world hunger everywhere
No child on this earth would ever go hungry anywhere
Medicine would be available to all who are ill
It would not matter the costs, it's would be Gods will.

Years ago back in Biblical times, children were taken care of
By their fathers and mothers whom they dearly loved
Nowadays half the children have no parents to go to
Which I think is really sad, what they go through.

Linda Laybolt
Whispers From Heaven

I would put an end to child abuse, that would be against the law
Those who would not report would be guilty too of what they saw
I would end all the wars and fighting within all countries everywhere
It may take time but Gods love would be exalt the nasty particles of air.

There would be no more killings of any kind whatsoever
Killing has to stop for this world to get better
Imagine your , brother, father or son or daughter not going off to war
A dream every mother dreams of, is that too much to ask for?

What about the elderly who get tossed aside all the time?
Widows in some places are scorned and left to starve.
What is wrong with their families, they can't take care of them?
Do they not forget, she raised them from birth, they are her kin?

What about the poor young brides that get stoned to death in this modern age?
While the rest of family sit and watch her husband in total rage?
What has happened here, where is Gods Love Where did it go?
God made woman a special heart full of compassion, this is so!

Another thing Iwould change is abortion of all Gods Precious little ones
Do they not realize God sent them from Heaven, His daughters and sons!"
But then again when you think of it, its fair to say
We are all Children Of God, in every possible way!

All the money that is wasted on space shuttles and wars
It sickens me and my heart breaks while earths inhibitants are pushed outdoors
Where is the humanity that was placed in Mens hearts as well in womans?
Mind you, not all men are alike but there are alot out there full of evil in the lands.

Linda Laybolt
Whispers From Heaven

You say well its Satan dragging us down, but we all were given free will
I know for a fact it exists to this very modern day still
But take notice all through the years, its mostly been bad men who drug this world down
Satan is having a great laugh everywhere he goes, the world round and round.

Woman on the other side have a warm, compassionate heart
No matter what is thrown at us, it will never break apart
So why should we have sit sit back and let men rule over us
When the only one that should be ruling, All Nations is the Lord Jesus.

There are so many evil people out there, so much money wasted today
It has to stop somewhere; someone has to the message throughout the air
Nothing else seems to work, so why not make it worldwide with this message
And send it to everyone you know, no matter their age.

I am not saying Let's get rid of all men by any means
As there are alot of good ones out there too so it seems.
All we have to do is retrain the ones to know God
And all our problems will be forever solved!

But Ladies, don't you all agree, if we had the chance
Maybe the world would learn to love, sing and dance!
Instead of this bickering and hatred going on
Then maybe all humans would find happiness and get along.

Now there is only one part left to this poem
And that is the goal to bring everyone Home
Home to Our Mighty Lord in Heaven Above
Home to be eternally filled with His Everlasting Love!

Remember Yesterday.....

Remember yesterday,
When we were once young, full of play
The world was ours, not a care to worry about
We'd run and jump till we were all played out!

Getting up and going to school
Not missing a day was the Golden Rule
Walking the long road there in rain and snow
No matter what, we had to go!

Recess and lunchtime, we all got to play
Outside of course, was there any other way?
When the school bell rang for us to go in
We knew school books waited for us within.

There was no computers back then
Just paper, crayons. pencils with no pen
We paid fully attention to what our teacher said
Or across our desk came the yardstick instead!

Sure now and again, we'd play pranks on the teacher
Only to find out, she was a real mean creature.
Standing all day in the corner was not fun
Or getting the strap, one by one!

But then again, things always weren't all that bad
We all learned to write on that writing pad!
We learned everything we needed to know
In that one room school house, many years ago!

Now when I look back, I am grateful for all we had
It may not have been much but I am Glad
We learned to respect each other and get along
Which wasn't so bad, am I wrong?

The Lords Prayer was said everyday
Not cast away like today!
The Lord was part of our school
Why did they change the rule and be so cruel?

Come Sit With Me, Beside Still Waters

Come sit beside still waters with me
Rest your weary soul, I will stay with thee.
Be not consumed by burdens you bare
Give them to me, for I really do care.
If you feel lost & don't know what to do
Remember I am here, always to come to.
Do not waste thoughts on fear of the unknown
This day is almost over, you were never left alone.
The sun is making its way to rest for another day
Slowly darkness appears to be on its way.
Do not be afraid, of what the night might bring
There is nothing to fear at all, not a thing.
The moon and stars dazzle across the skies
Lay back your head, rest those weary eyes.
Take comfort in knowing that I am here with you
Protecting and watching over all you say and do.
I am Jesus your loving Lord and your friend
You are my Child and I will love you always, till the very end.

He Is God

He is God, Creator of All, the Earth and Heavens Above
He is God, The Great Alpha and Omega, Full of Love.
He is God, Nothing on this earth can take Him away
He is God, He reigns forever and is here to stay.
He is God, What Was, Is and Yet to Be
He is God, He is My Lord, My Saviour that died for me.
He is God, He will not be trampled upon or taken down
He is God, He is Greater than anything that is around.

He is God, Many have tried to get rid of Him
He is God, Many realize He is too Mighty for them.
He is God, Many try to discredit Him and all His wonders
He is God, Only to discover, we are all sisters and brothers.
He is God, He loved us first and always will
He is God, He has a Master Plan for us to fulfill.
He is God, He is my Comfort, Strength and Lord
He is God, He is Not To Be Ignored.
He is God, He cannot be erased, He is our history
He is God, He is Real and not just a made up story.
He is God, He made me and you and all we see
He is God, We are His Family, check out the family tree.
He is God, Full of compassion, strength and forgiving
He is God, His Love will always be Everlasting to Everlasting.
He is God, He is Jesus, He is the Holy Spirit, All Three
He is God, Alpha and Omega, The Great Almighty!
But most important, He is my Father in Heaven Above
Who watches over me, filling my heart with His Divine Love!

My House Is My Home

Every church you see, is my house
The doors are always open for you to come in
No one is ever refused to come into my home
All are welcome, especially my children that are living in sin.
When I said, Come to me, I am the Way
This message for meant for all of mankind
Not for the selected few or chosen ones
But for all, no one is to be left behind.
My house can be seen in every city or town in the world
Even the smallest village has one of my homes
Some may be huge like the one in Rome
Others may look different, with high domes.
Some may not even look like a church at all
They may be a building carrying my name
Some may be old abandoned churches left for years
But they are still my houses, just the same.
Somewhere out there, there stands a house

Not just any house, but My Home
It sits there day after day, waiting for you to come in
So I can say to you, My Child, Welcome Home!

My Lord Will Hear When I Call Upon Him

I said to myself, I am all alone
But I heard a voice whisper, you are never alone!
I am always here by your side, I see all you do
I am here waiting, with open arms for you!
I can see into your heart, when it is torn apart
I can see the sadness in your eyes, before the tears start
I see the long lonely paths that you walk from day to day
But I am with you, I am never far away.
I see the good times, the laughter and the love
Even though, my home is in Heaven Above.
When you come to me for comfort, I am always there
I hear the sincerity and humility in your voice, in prayer.
I hear you talk to me all the time, throughout the day
I never get bored at listening to what you say.
There are many times, I have been with you that you did not know
Those times, I carried you when you were feeling low.
I have wrapped my loving arms around you, when you had fear
And stayed with you through it, I know you felt me near.
You are My Child and I will always love you
And your heart tells me, that you love me too!
I lifted up my head in shame, for I am never alone
For the Lord is My Shepherd and He never leaves His flock on their own!

Count your blessings,
each and everyday
Be grateful unto the Lord
when you pray.

Rain will fall on many days
but the sun will return again
Be grateful for all days,
not just every now and then.

Whispers From Heaven

Trials and tribulations may follow you
some of the time
That mountain in front of you
may look abit harder to climb.

When you feel that
you can no longer go on
Ask the Lord for strength,
to keep moving along.

Sometimes you may feel like giving up,
but that is not Gods plan
He put you here for a reason,
that perhaps you will never understand.

Have no fear, you are never alone;
The Lord is always beside you
He will never forsake you,
He will be there to see you through.

At the end of this long journey
that has come your way
Remember, who has helped you
and guided you each and every day.

Give thanks unto the Lord
for always being there, day and night
Count your blessings and be grateful
With God by your side, everything will be all right.

Believe And He Will Come

I struggle with fear, not knowing the pain
I will have with all the tests
Sometimes, I feel so alone
Scared and depressed.

Linda Laybolt
Whispers From Heaven

I sit quietly and start to pray
For the Lord Jesus to come to me, on this day.
I look around at all the people
Sitting here in the waiting room
No one speaks or smiles, sadness lingers here
Just grim faces, full of despair and gloom.
The look in their eyes tells it all
Most are full of fear of the unknown
In silence, we all sit and wait
Wishing we could leave and go back home.
As names get called, one by one
We know soon, ours will be too
We watch as more patients keep arriving
Wondering if they too feel, what we are going through.
Finally, my name gets called out
A nurse smiles saying, come this way
Down to a room with CatScan written the door
They put an IV in my arm on this day.
As I lay on the cold table, waiting for the scan to start
They tell me the test does not take long
Lights are revolving back and forth around me
I feel scared, thinking this is not where I belong.
I start to pray to Jesus to give me comfort
My heart cries to Him, to come and rescue me
All of a sudden, I am filled with warmth inside
I open my eyes and The Lord, I clearly see.
He is laying beside me, inside the catscan
His arms are wrapped around me, no longer do I fear
The smile on His face gives me great comfort
I feel safe as He holds me, close and near.
There is a Light glowing all around Him
I cannot speak but I feel His Divine Love embrace me
Whatever happens now, I no longer have to worry
My Lord Jesus will be with me to face, whatever is to be.

Linda Laybolt
Whispers From Heaven

My Angel

As I look out from across the deck
I see the sun rising above the ocean
And the waves rolling slowly to the shore
As I walk down the deck into my garden
I gaze and stare at all the beauty there
Within all the different colours of flowers and trees.
As I listen, I hear the sound of a harp faintly
Drifting into my ears
Like an angel playing softly and beautiful upon a harp.
Makes one wonder as to why God created the angels
Including the ones that watch over us
Day in and day out never ceasing to guard over us
Even though we may not see them, they are all around us
God has sent them to watch over us
When our final breath here on earth is done
They are there to carry us Home to God in the Heavens above.
So if we only learned to believe and pray to God up above
The angels will be there for us always.

By John

In The Arms Of An Angel, I Awake

In the arms of an angel, I awake
She is my guardian angel, no mistake
She is smiling down at me, full of love
My Guardian Angel sent from Heaven Above.
In the arms of an angel, Fly Me Away
In the arms of my angel, take me Home to stay!

So you've lived your life, the best you could do
But the wheels of fate has turned, your days left now are few
The years have quickly fled by, where did they go?
Things that seem like yesterday, are now years ago.
Memories are all these days, that you carry in your heart
Tucked away in that special place, they will never part.

Linda Laybolt
Whispers From Heaven

In the arms of an angel, I awake
She is my Guardian Angel, no mistake
She is smiling down at me, full of love
My Guardian Angel sent from Heaven Above.
In the arms of an angel, Fly Me Away
In the arms of my angel, take me Home to stay!

There are times when, I just stare into space
And Thank God in Heaven, for His Loving Embrace
There are times when, I close my weary eyes
And dream about beyond, the clear blues skies
These are the times, I visualize Heaven in my mind
And leave all of my troubles far behind.

In the arms of an angel, I awake
She is my guardian angel, no mistake
She is smiling down at me, full of love
My Guardian Angel sent from Heaven Above.
In the arms of an angel, Fly Me Away
In the arms of my angel, take me Home to stay!

There are times when I think about you My Lord
And how much you are so Loved and Adored
These are the times, I am so thankful to you
For loving me, no matter what I do.
These are the times, I feel Your love surround me
I am never alone, I am so grateful to thee.

In the arms of an angel, I awake
She is my guardian angel, no mistake
She is smiling down at me, full of love
My Guardian Angel sent from Heaven Above.
In the arms of an angel, Fly Me Away
In the arms of my angel, take me Home to stay!

Linda Laybolt
Whispers From Heaven

The Lord's Free Will

Lord, It is my will with reverence, to bow down and pray
Whenever I want, for you are with me, night and day
I know you are there, as I can feel your presence beside me
Even though when I look around, I cannot see thee!

Lord, it is my will to talk to you anytime I feel like it
Even if its a whole lot of words or just a little bit
Sometimes, when I am driving, I tend to ramble on
I think you don't mind it, I hope I am right and not wrong!

Lord, it is my will to call upon you when I need you
Especially, if I happen to be really sad and blue
For you always come and give me comfort within
Compassion is yours now and always has been!

Lord, it is my will to put my faith and trust in you
My hopes and dreams go along with that too
My thoughts are yours as you hear everything
I can't carry a tune, a closed ear I don't mind, when I sing!

Lord, it is my will to come to you for strength
I heard you are never far away, always at arm's length
I believe that this is really true with all my heart
For you always seem to lift me up, when I fall apart!

Lord, it is my will to love, honor and obey your commands
It is my will to walk with you, please don't ever let go of my hand
Thank you, Lord, for giving me the choice of free will
Without it, my life would have been completely downhill!

Lord, it is my will to love you above all forevermore
Without you, I'd be lost, my heart would be tore
Lord, it was your will to come rescue me from sin
Everyday I live, I will thank you from deep within!

Lord of Heaven, King of Kings, it is my will to be with you
My Dear Lord Jesus, always keep me within view
My free will brought me to you, because of your Divine Love
Forever, let me be your humble servant in, Your Mighty Kingdom in Heaven Above!

Jesus Walked On Water

On a boat in the Sea of Galilee, the disciples set sail
Little did they know, a raging storm was about to prevail!
As they slept, the storms wind and waves caused must discontent
Even though with the sea, this was a natural event!

When they awoke, all were filled with much fear
Thoughts that the boat may capsize, was perfectly clear!
What were they going to do, they were on their own
Jesus had gone to pray on the mountainside, his return unknown!

But in the midst of the storm, Jesus appears to them
Walking on water towards the boat, they do not believe it is Him!
Afraid that they are seeing a ghost, Jesus tells them, Take courage
It is I, Don't be afraid, even thought the storm continued to rage!

Peter replies, Tell me to come into the water, Lord, if it is you
So Jesus invites Peter to enter the water, out of the blue!
Peter starts to walk toward Jesus, his eyes focused only on Him
But then he looks down at the waves, starts to sink, all is grim!

Then Peter cries out to Jesus, what else was he to do
Jesus immediately reached out His hand, for Peter to cling to!
As they get into the boat, the storm begins to cease
The waves and water are once again at peace!

Truly, you are the Son Of God, Peter says to Jesus
I am sure, he thought to himself, only God could save us!
When Peter had glanced away from Jesus, he began to sink
This makes a person want to stop and really think!

Linda Laybolt
Whispers From Heaven

The disciples did not recognize Jesus at first, as he walked
Even though they spent much time with Him, their eyesight was blocked!
Jesus walked on water to save His Beloved Disciples, in the raging sea
Just like he died on the cross, for you and me!

When the storm is raging, the waves are gushing all around you
Will you recognize Jesus, when he comes to your rescue?
Will you reach out for his hand, when he reaches to save you?
Or will you turn away afraid, not knowing what to do?

Fall Will Soon Be Gone

The beauty of fall can be seen here, there and everywhere
When God made this season, it was done with loving care.
Shades of yellows and reds spread throughout the trees
The warmth of summer is now a cool harsh breeze.

The old white owl sits and watches his friends
Hustling back and forth, as fall transcends.
Leaves are falling fast now to the ground
Everything is changing fast, as he looks around.

Most of the animals are preparing for winter to come
While others are still enjoying playing in the sun.
Most of the birds have taken flight to warmer places
Others search for shelter in closed small spaces.

Some salmon make their last run up the river to spawn
Even though they die, the next generation will still live on.
The bears find a den to hibernate the winter away
The deer, moose and others will stick it out and stay.

Some will head to the city or a small town
In search for some food to be found.
But somehow, they all seem to survive
God provides for them, keeping them alive.

Linda Laybolt
Whispers From Heaven

The old white owl sits proud perched in the trees
Glancing around at all the wonders he sees.
He looks carefully at all the beauty in his sight
He knows exactly that everything is just perfectly right!

Share Your Memories...

Memories are yours, some are good while some are bad
Some are full of laughter, while some are really sad.
Each day is a new beginning of things to come
But remaining in the past lingers for some.

Things to happen today reflect our everyday lives
While important things of yesterdays gone by survives.
The important things, we must never let it disappear
We must keep it close to our hearts, forever near.

We have to keep on telling the story about Jesus
Our Beloved Saviour, who died for us.
We must never let the world forget
That Jesus died paying mankind's debt.

We cannot let the world forget how Jesus was born
Descending from the Throne of Heaven, where He was greatly adorn.
We must tell others about His teachings of His Heavenly Father
His Loving Ways, His Miraculous Healings, and His Walking on Water.

We must always hold the Cross of Jesus, close and near
And spread His Word to all, without fear.
His greatest commandment was "To Love One Another"
Love everyone as you would your sister and brother.

Memories can be a great thing, especially if it is a good one
So don't forget to share the one of God's Chosen Son!
Lord of Lords, King of Kings, Forever He Will Reign
May The Lord Jesus Forever In Our Hearts Remain!

Linda Laybolt
Whispers From Heaven

A Soldier Never Dies....

The sounds of guns are always close and near
But a brave soldier shows no fear
I'll stand up and fight for you my friend
Right until the bitter end.

We stand proud and strong, alongside each other
Fighting for our country, one after another
We have all left our families behind
To fight for the better of mankind.

Once I was reluctant to leave you all behind
But nowadays, all I feel is peace of mind.
I've lived a life full of laughter and tears
Made many good friends throughout the years.

My family here on earth means the world to me
But I have another family that I long to see
Somewhere beyond the deep blue sky
Heaven awaits, in the blink of an eye.

When the end is near and the time is right
I'll bid farewell, without a fight.
The birds will sing in the trees
My heart and soul will be at ease.

With God walking beside us, we will always win
The battle may take us, but our souls belong to Him.
As a band of brothers, we will remain
Soldiers in Heavens Army, under Gods domain.

The Battles Of Aging

Its been extra lonely these days, with you not here
Sometimes, I think the pain is too hard to bare.
Yesterday may be the past and gone forever
But my heart continually says, Never! Never!

It's funny how life just drifts by before your eyes
The older you get, the faster time flies.
It seems like yesterday that I was a young and innocent
Today, I'm looked at as being old and ancient.

Linda Laybolt
Whispers From Heaven

Yesterday we were all together and having fun
Today, I am left all alone, with really noone.
I had friends and family galore to talk to
But that was yesterday, today very few.

Everyone thinks its great to live a long life and be old
I wish I had someone, like old days to take me and hold.
It's not much fun when you know more deceased people than alive
Sometimes, I ask God why He is making me survive?

The friends I do have left, I can count on one hand
Some still know me, some don't; do you understand?
They have been tossed aside also by family and friends
Alone and forsaken, just like odds and ends.

Old age is not the greatest, not by any means these days
Times have changed for the worst, in so many ways.
When I was young, older people got respect and taken care of
The dying were surrounded by family, they could feel the love.

Nowadays, noone has time for you, thats the way it goes
You are just an acquaintance, that everyone knows.
But I guess that is just the way, things were meant to be
Is it just me and my way of thinking, or do you also see?

But as despressing as this may seem to be to you
I have My Lord Jesus, My Saviour to get me through.
Most days are spent, talking to Him in Heaven Above
Someday soon, I will return to Him and the ones that I dearly love!

The Long Path To Home

Once I was a little girl running and playing
Jumping in and out of puddles, dancing in the rain
Running through open fields of wild flowers
It seemed a child, forever I would remain.
But that was yesterday.........

Linda Laybolt
Whispers From Heaven

Once I was a teenager listening to all my favorite songs
Talking on the phone for endless hours to my friends
Drawing hearts with initials of boys within them
Carefully perserving my box of keepsakes, of odds and ends.
But that was yesterday..........

Once I was a young woman who searched the world for love
Saying "I Do" to the man who had won my heart
Reaching out to hold the hand of the man I truly loved
Promising to love, honor and obey, till death do us part.
But that was yesterday...........

Once I was a young mother of three little children
The days were so long that never seemed to end
Trying to teach them right from wrong
Life revolved around them, sometimes they were my only friend.
But that was yesterday..........

Now, I am old and grey with grandchildren to enjoy
I sit back and watch them run and play with my heart full of love
The years have so quickly passed by me
I spend most days reading of The Good Lord Above.
But this is today.........

I know in my heart the day will soon come
When He will come for me to go, Home to Heaven above
My work here on earth is finally over, my soul will be at peace
Knowing I am Forever Embraced by His Eternal Love!
This is my future........

Field Of Dreams

There is a pasture beyond the meadows
That I often go to, to ponder the day away.
On a warm sunny day, you'll find me there
Nestled under the big oak, with no cares for the day.

Linda Laybolt
Whispers From Heaven

This is my place of solitude, my field of dreams
Here I can dream the day away and wish of things to be.
No worries or sorrow ever exist here
In my field of dreams, all burdens are set free.

As I set back and watch all the beauty that surrounds me
I give thanks to the Lord for bringing me here.
This is our own little private place that we talk
In my field of dreams, Gods love is seen everywhere.

All is perfect and serene in my field of dreams
Little girls and boys play amongst the wild flowers, for hours on end.
Angels fly through the air watching the children & playing to
Sometimes a unicorn will appear, looking to meet a new friend.

And uunder the old oak tree, we watch with great ease
As the trees sway back and forth to the little birds lullabies.
Even the flowers seem to dance gracefully to the music
Everything seems so magical, under the bright blue sky.

And when it's time for me to go home as it is getting late
I know I'll be back again soon, that's no mistake.
My field of dreams will be always waiting for me
And so will my Lord in Heaven to let my spirit run free.

I Heard Her Cry

Amongst the crowd, I heard the womans cries
When she became visible, tears filled my eyes.
There stood a middle aged woman all alone
Whom to most people, Mary was very well known.

I wondered what all the shouting was all about
So I decided to go and check it out.
And there He was walking through the crowd
As they shouted obsene words at Him out loud.

Linda Laybolt
Whispers From Heaven

My heart ached to see Him, it was so inhumane
Beaten and bruised, He was in so much pain.
As He dragged a cross along on His weak back
I wondered why My Master Jesus was under attack?

I walked along among the crowd that day
Even though my heart kept saying, run away.
Why was only Jesus's mother in sight?
Had all the Disciples and Followers taken flight?

Sadly Jesus was nailed to the cross for all to view
They shouted loudly, "King of the Jews"
As they placed a crown of thorns upon His Head
But not a tear did Jesus shed!

Instead, Jesus prayed to His Father in Heaven
For what they had done, would be forgiven.
In the end, only a few followers stood by His side
Not forsaking their Master, to run and hide!

The Beauty Of Creation

All living things slowly awakes, a new day has begun
The water looks like it is dancing, as it sparkles from the sun
The little birds sing high up in the trees, for all to hear
Flowers gently open their stems,to show off the beauty they bare!

The morning dew and mist that filled the air, lingers on for awhile
A feeling of anew fills my soul, which brings to me, a smile
As a new day, a new morning, descends upon the earth
Just like many years ago, in the first days of its birth!

The trees slightly sway from the soft breeze, that brushes against my face
Two swans swim by, full of tranquility and grace
There is so much beauty everywhere, to be found
As I patiently take the time, to look around!

Linda Laybolt
Whispers From Heaven

When God created the earth, he did so with so much care
Everything came from a heart of love, most willing to share
For all we see and feel, before our very own eyes
Was created for us by Him, the perfect Paradise!

It does not matter where you go, there's beauty everywhere to see
They say Paradise was lost, how can this possibly be?
People nowadays still search for this so-called lost Holy Place
But I often wonder, is it not standing right before our face?

Could it possibly be, that Paradise has been here with us all along?
And that somehow, mankind got confused, and got it all wrong?
Awesome and Wondrous, are the works of My God, Creator of all things
What you have given us, so much happiness and love, to the soul it brings!

It does not matter what it is, there is beauty in everything to behold
The love in your heart, over and over is told
With so much splendor and glamor, made out of love
I cannot even think to imagine, what it is like in your Great Kingdom, in Heaven Above!

A Prayer Of Love

Take my hand, hold it tight within yours
Shine your light of love, upon me forevermore
Stay close beside me, protect me from all harm
Be my refuge, safe within your arms!

Keep me within your sight, always within full view
The road of righteousness is the road that I must pursue!
For I am not perfect, sin is hiding behind every turn
I don't want to step on a path, that leads to no return!

Linda Laybolt
Whispers From Heaven

For there will be times, that I will stray
Those are the times, I need you to find my way
Stay with me through this life, each and every day
Wrapped within your love, don't ever go away!

You are my foundation, my rock that I lean on
You are my strength, when called upon
Pick me up when I stumble and fall, rescue me
When darkness falls, be my guiding light, for me to see!

My life is yours, I give it willingly to you
Your unconditional love is all I need, to see me through
Holy, Holy, Holy, Lord God Almighty
What was, is and is to come! Forever, I will love thee!

My Forgiving Lord

Forgive me Lord, for I have sinned
Sadness now lurks, from deep within
I try to live by your Word, each day
But sometimes from you, I do slip away.

I don't plan on these things to be
I know I can't hide things, from thee
It seems wrong decisions are made, time after time
And the sin I committ, is all mine.

Why is it so hard to do as you ask and obey?
And live according to your plan everyday
Every now and then I slip up, I know I am to blame
It fills my heart with sadness, along with the shame.

Time and time again, I come to you in prayer
To ask for forgiveness, in earnest despair
Time and time again, you never turn me away
Even though, I have let myself be lead astray.

Linda Laybolt
Whispers From Heaven

You are such a Loving God, in each and every way
Even in my darkest hours, you are never far away
With open arms, you are there to comfort me
To take my sins, once again, setting my spirit free.

Your unconditional love, I feel deep within my soul
Surrounds my heart, making me feel whole
My Heavenly Father, you are the one who truly cares
Only you have the answers to all my prayers.

I am so grateful for being a child of yours
I cannot promise that I will not sin anymore
But I will honestly try to abide in your ways
Each and everyday.

Lastly, I just want to say Lord, thank you so much
For always letting me feel, you Heavenly touch
Thank you for giving me, your Divine Love
My Precious, Forgiving Lord, In Heaven above!

Hallelujah

HEAVEN is what all men seek, humble and meek
ACCEPT the Lord in your heart, forever to stay and never to depart
LIVE a life in the Lord Almighty, so all can see
LIFT your hands in prayer, way up high in the air
EXALT and glorify the King of Heaven, in Him all things are given
LOVE never fails, only through the Lord it prevails
UNFAILING is the Lord, your God in His love for you, to see you through
JUST put your trust in the Lord forever, the Lord promises to deliver
ALWAYS the Lord God is with you, His love is always true
HEAVEN is the Lord's throne, and yours too, for you are one of His own!

Hallelujah, Praise The Lord!

I Love How You Love

I love how you love me
Forever, I want to stay with thee!
And I will shout it from the top of the trees
I love how you love me!

I love how you are always there
Anytime, any place, anywhere!
All I have to do is talk to you
And you're love comes shining through!

I love how you walk beside me
And beside me, you will always be!
I love knowing that when I can't go on, and you will agree
You lift me up Lord, and carry me!

I love how you comfort me, when I am feeling blue
You're always there when I need you, to turn to!
I love how wipe any tears I may have, away
And knowing your endless love, is here to stay!

I love how you protect me, day and night
And when it's dark, you shine on me, your guiding light!
And when I feel lonely, your closeness is within my sight
Safe within your loving arms, everything is alright!

I love how you have touched my heart
With you, I will always be and never depart!
I love how you gave your life so willingly for me
I thank you Lord, for setting my sins free!

I love how you love me
Forever, I will stay with thee!
My Lord Jesus, I love how you love me
For now and all eternity!

Linda Laybolt
Whispers From Heaven

Wrapped within your precious love, forevermore
You are my Lord that I completely adore
King of Kings, you reign the earth and the Heavens above
My Lord Jesus, I love how you love!

A Message From God To You

As God sits on His Mighty Throne, He listens to you
He sees and hears everything that you do.
He sees the tears that fall from your eyes
He hears the sounds of all the babies cries.

He wonders why He gets asked so many times in vain
Where are you God? Can you not feel my pain?
Why God did you do this to this to me?
Was I not as faithful to you as I could be?

Why won't you stop the needless killings going on?
Yet, you say You have been with us all along!
Why would you take my innocent child away?
Why do you let the suffering continue from day to day?

Where are the miracles at? I need to know!
Where are you God? Where is the Almighty God of long ago?
God looks down from Heaven Above and replies,"I Am Here"
I have always been here and I Am Everywhere!

Everything bad that happens, I get the blame
Yet noone down there, has no remorse or shame.
Do you not remember how my children suffered through the years?
There were many hardships and turmoils, so many tears.

I give you miracles everyday, yet you are too blind to see
Everyday I send life but little babies are sent back to me.
Man has changed the world I created for you
Once was paradise is now full of smog, with no sky to view.

Linda Laybolt
Whispers From Heaven

Cities are so huge with no room to move for anyone
Buildings erected in the sky, shaded areas where there should be sun.
Many animals and plants have become extinct, because of the modern age
People have changed over the years, hearts are now full of rage.

Rockets soar into the sky, sattelites circle the earth everyday
Nations keep close eye on each other, incase a bomb is sent their way.
Why is so much money spent on modern technology to advance
When children die from hunger and disease without a fighting chance.

What about the homeless people you meet on the street?
Broken souls, just looking for a place to sleep and something to eat.
Everyday there is threat of war, my children die needlessly
Terrorists live to kill and torture, problems are never settled peacefully!

Every country wants to rule and be number one in this modern day
Nation leaders have forgotten that I rule and I Am The Way!
I am here, I have always been here; I see everything
Some of my children have turned away, never listening to anything.

I did my best when I created a world for mankind to live in
But lately, all I see is people living with tormented hearts and in sin.
I even sent you my Beloved Son Jesus to teach about me "Your Father"
He gave you the greatest commandment "To Love One Another!"

Yet, you turned on Him; and nailed Him to an old wooden cross
What more do I have to do to get my point across?
Yes indeed, I hear all prayers; I listen carefully to each word that is said
Sometimes, it takes awhile for me to answer but I Am Not Dead.

Each and everyone of you, when you were born, I had a plan
It's been that way since I created your world and life began!
It is not my fault if you choose not to listen to me, when I talk
Or that you have chosen a different path in life to walk!

I do have many children that are very humble and loyal to me
But I still love each of you the same way, yet this you cannot see!
Like I said before, when you were born I have a plan for each of you
Some of you will live long lives, others not; this is true.

So don't be sad or blame me when a loved one is taken from you
It's all part of the bigger plan that I have chosen so don't be blue!
My angels are always with you night and day
Protecting and guiding you, along the way!

You are never alone for I am always here watching you too
No matter what the outcome is, they are my plans for you!
I Am ...The Great I Am...
Alpha and Omega....The Beginning and The End
I am still here...The God Of Abraham!

Loving one another is not such a hard thing to do
After all, I should know; I AM YOUR FATHER AND I LOVE YOU!

Song Of The Morning

It's early morn as I watch the sunrise
Night has departed saying goodbye
As I set on my porch looking around
I hear little birds singing their song.

A robin sits quietly on a branch as it sings
Such happiness to my heart that it brings.
Soon the others all join in harmony
Like a choir of angels, how can this be?

Every morning there voices can be heard
Yet they cannot speak, not even a word.
I wonder do they hear something from the sky
Do they hear the angels in Heaven, up high?

Linda Laybolt
Whispers From Heaven

Watching closely, they all seem to look above
As they sing their lullably, filled with love.
Do they hear or see something that we cannot?
Singing to the Lord is a wonderful thought!

So next time you hear the little birds sing
Remind yourself, they're singing to our King.
Remember, The Lord hears and sees everything we do
So He hears and sees the little birds too!

Dear Lord

Dear Lord,
Watch over me each and every day
Always be here to stay
Keep me from all harm
Safe within your arms
Be my refuge when I need you
Be there to see me through
All the paths that I walk upon
Dear Lord I pray, my whole lifelong!

You are my candle light
That glows in the darkness of night
A light that''s so divine
That never dies but forever shines
Keep it lit, within my sight
Morning, noon and night
Don't ever let it fade away
Dear Lord, this I truly pray!

Keep me within your endless love
My Precious Lord, in Heaven above
My heart will always be yours
You are the one that I adore
Watch over me, each and every day
Living in your righteous ways
A child of yours, I will always be
Dear Lord I pray, forever stay with me!

God Loves You And So Do I!

Give praise to the Lord all day long
Let your heart sing out in song
Talk to Him throughout your day
Always, let Him lead the way!
Remember God loves you and so do I
As He sits on His Mighty Throne, way up high!

Sometimes things may not go as you planned
You question why but you don't understand
When God closes a door, it is not the end
Another door awaits, around the bend.
Remember God loves you and so do I
As He sets on His Mighty Throne, way up high!

Never feel like you are all alone and on your own
Never be afraid of the future or the unknown
God is by your side day and night
Watching over you, keeping you in full sight!
Remember God loves you and so do I
As He sits on His Mighty Throne, way up high!

As each day passes, God Blessings fall upon you
No matter what, you are going through
Take a look around you, and you will find
Blessings galore of every kind!
Remember God loves you and so do I
As He sits from His Mighty Throne, way up high!

God has a special plan for you
He sees and hears everything you do
He knows what He is doing from Heaven Above
As He sends down to you, His Heavenly Love.
Remember God loves you and so do I
As he sits on His Mighty Throne, way up high!

Jesus Loves Me

A little girl was walking along the road one day
All dressed pretty and prim as this was Sunday.
She was on her way to church as happy as could be
Taking her time, admiring all the sights that she could see.
It was a beautiful day, little voices echoed through the air
Little birds were singing everywhere.
As she walked she sang Jesus Loves Me, This I know
For the Bible tells me so!
Little ones do Him belong
They are weak but He is strong.
Yes, Jesus Loves me
Yes, Jesus Loves me
Yes, Jesus Loves me
The Bible tells me so.
I am sure all of us can relate to this from our own childhood
And this hymn, the meaning, we all understood!
But nowadays, we rarely hear this hymn sung
Have we forgotten, the teachings of when we were young?
As a child, we knew that Jesus loved us, there was no doubt
As an adult, He still does, day in and day out!
As a child, we all had pure hearts amongst all of us
As adults, some have lost their faith in Jesus!
Have they forgotten the hymn of not so long ago?
Jesus Loves Me, This I know
For the Bible tells me so!

A Child's Guardian Angel

This fighting and yelling
Makes me want to cry
I can feel the tears
As they start to fill my eyes.

Linda Laybolt
Whispers From Heaven

I am so scared
My tummy feels sick inside
I've got to find a place
Where I can run and hide.

You think that I don't understand
All the mean things that you say
Just because I am still small
You think that it's o.k.

I may not be able to talk much yet
But I can feel when things are not right
I just want you to love me
And hold me ever so close and tight.

You both say I am an accident
And was not meant to be
I don't understand these words
Maybe someday, you'll explain them to me.

You may think that I am all alone
But I have a secret friend
Who says she'll always stay with me
All of my life, till the very end.

She tells me lots of stories
That make me laugh and smile
I'm the only one who sees her
But that's to be for only a little while.

She told me to call her angel
For I cannot say her name
No matter what happens in life
She will always be with me and love me just the same.

She plays lots of games with me
And showed me how those funny white things make her fly
She gives me hugs and kisses as gently tucks me into bed
And sings to me something, she calls a sweet lullaby.

Linda Laybolt
Whispers From Heaven

She tells me stories of her home which she calls heaven
And draws pictures for me to see
Someday, I will take you there
But that is not for a longtime yet, to be.

She tells me about her father who's name is God
And Jesus,his only son
How he loves all little children
That I, too, am also a loved one.

She says the time is coming soon
That I will be loved, all the time
But until then, I will wrap my loving arms around you
Don't be afraid, for I am your guardian angel and things are going to be just fine.

There Are No Tears In Heaven

Yesterday I visited a friend who lives on the edge of town
When I got there the rain was pouring down
The old man was rocking back & forth in his rocking chair
He looked happy but a feeling of sadness engulfed the air.

The old man said I have been feeling great these last few days
So I've been giving the Good Lord lots of Praise..
I know my days left on earth are few
So there's something I want to give to you.

Sure I replied but you'll be just fine
Why look at you, you'd think you were on cloud nine!
So stop thinking bad thoughts
And don't become so distraught!

You see this Bible of mine that I read everyday
Well I don't need it anymore, I can honestly say
I want you to take it and read this sacred book
And read between the lines by taking a second look.

Linda Laybolt
Whispers From Heaven

It is the most precious gift that I have in my possession to give
It teaches you right from wrong and how the Good Lord wants you to live.
When the old man handed me His Bible, I had tears in my eyes
I never dreamed he would ever part with it, this was truly a surprise.

The old man saw my tears and stated to sing:
There are no tears in Heaven
All sins there are forgiven
Jesus paid the debt for all sins
That's where real life begins!
There are no tears in Heaven
Only Joy and Peace among the living
You wanted the truth so I'm letting you know
That the Good Lord in Heaven Loves you so!

A few days later, I received the word that the old man had died
I picked up His Precious Bible and broke down and cried.
Just then, I could hear the old man singing his favourite song
And before I knew it, I too was singing it every day, all day long!

Alone And Forsaken

Today a little baby is born, sent from Heaven above
Into a world of despair, often to a world without love!
Another one of God's precious children, to a life of sorrow
Another Child with no hopes of a brighter tomorrow!
To a place where it is a struggle from day to day
To a place where there is never any hopes of getting away!
Maybe this child will grow into adulthood, maybe not
Most times, these children from society are long forgot!
Often, they are left on their own to survive in the early years
Often their young life is filled with only so many tears!
Sometimes, they end up losing both parents, left all alone
Or with other siblings hungry and sick, struggling on their own!
Living a life going through rotten garbage, for something to eat
We see them helpless, worldwide begging on the streets!

Or they may be in some corner of the globe, in a remote place
In a shack struggling from day to day, forgotten by the human race!
With very few clothes to wear, no one seems to care
About God's Little Children, that can be found everywhere!
Most die from hunger or sickness, help for them is too late
In this modern world, children die needlessly, to this very date!
Why is that we can send a man to the moon, fight war after war
Yet we cannot make sure that every child is fed, is it too much to ask for?
The money that is wasted in every country around
Yet childrens cries for help, are still to be found!
These little children did not ask to be brought into a world of despair
It's up to us to change, All God's Children need tender, loving care!
It is time for all governments worldwide, to set their priorities straight
These helpless children are our future, act now before it is too late!

Always Remember Jesus Loved The Little Children!
Matthew19:14

Heavenly Father's Heart Of Love

Thoughts keep pondering, around in my mind
About God and his relationship, to mankind
The Bible says he created us in his very own image
In Genesis, it's there, in the first chapter on the second page!

This really is something, to stop and think about
The Word of the Lord is true, beyond any doubt
As Mighty and Supreme God The Father is, in Heaven above
It must have broken his heart, to prove to us his Love!

I could never imagine giving up my own son for others
Even though we are taught as Christians, to love one another
Just thinking about it, brings tears to my eyes
Only Heavenly Father could hear, the weeping of his hearts cries!

Linda Laybolt
Whispers From Heaven

All through the Bible, the examples are written with care
Read between the fine lines, you will find them there
Most of our characteristics come from only one blood line
The Master who created us, Our Most Holy Father Divine!

It's so sad to think, let alone try to comprehend why
Mankind turned its back on its Creator, refusing to abide by
Heavenly Father gave them everything, we now see plus more
Ungrateful with hearts of stone, His Love for them shunned and ignored!

It's never talked how Heavenly Father felt, about how he was mistreated
But I think his heart somehow, must have been brokenhearted
I say this because we are so much like him in our ways
After all, he's our Loving Father, who created us in the first days!

Heavenly Father, Our Most Gracious Loving Lord, The Almighty
Still felt so much love for us, how could this possibly be
Sent to us the Messiah, His Beloved Most Holy Son, Jesus
To pave the road to Heaven, for all of us!

Jesus, Our Beloved Saviour who paid the ultimate price, for our sins
Carried and shared Heavenly Father's Love for us, from deep within
Not only did Our Lord Jesus suffer on the the cross that day
Heavenly Father in Heaven, I believe also suffered just as much, in every which way!

Memories

Nestled deep inside my heart
Are precious memories, from way back when
Some are happy, some are sad
Appearing out of nowhere, every now and then!
Memories are such a big part of life
Reflections of, days and events gone by
The past, moments of time never to return

Linda Laybolt
Whispers From Heaven

Yet forever staying within reach, closeby!
As we rise each day, to a new dawn
It is almost like starting life anew
Change is always on the horizon
What memories will this day bring to you?
It kind of makes a person wonder
About the great master plan, God had in mind
When He created, a new day, for each day
Another gift of love, for all of mankind!
For without this glorious new day
No new memories would be made
Life would be the same old boring ritual
No precious moments, ever to be displayed!
Next time, you are reflecting about the past
Take a moment to think of God's love
For without His great love for you
You would have no memories, to think of!

Can I Walk With You?

Precious Lord, My Dear Saviour
Can I walk along with you?
I"ll follow you, wherever you go
For as long as you will let me to!

I promise that I will listen close
To all that you have to say
A child who wants to learn
That is, what I am today!

I hear your voice so full of love
Precious Lord, how I believe you
You speak of so many things
That I must pursue!

Whispers From Heaven

Your words are so precious
To my very soul
That without you, in my life
I'm no longer complete and whole!

Precious Jesus, how your love shines
From deep within you
Obeying your Father
Tells me, your love is divine and true!

A shepherd you once were
A teacher for all to see
A healer of the sick and ill
And My Dear Saviour, who came to save me!

I cried out to you for help
And I bowed down in prayer
My Sweet Lord Jesus answered
With the Loving words, I care!

Forever, I will follow you
You are in my heart to stay
My Precious Lord Jesus
I became a Child of yours today!

The Lights Of Our Lord

Look up to the stars and take a good look around
And some of God's greatest wonders can be found
Lights twinkling all throughout the endless sky
If you are lucky, a shooting star will glide by!

The full moon shines big and bright
Full of beauty and much delight
Placed perfectly in the sky for us to see
Giving light at night to those on land and sea!

Linda Laybolt
Whispers From Heaven

As the lights of night start to disappear
The light of day slowly begins to appear
Sitting back in the sky, millions of miles away
The sun fills the earth with the warmth of its rays!

Rain or shine, snow, sleet or hail
The sun's light will resurface, without fail
Rising in the east and sitting in the west
Illuminating without ever taking rest!

Round and round the earth rotates every day
The light of day meets the lights of night halfway
Day after day, the same scenario is portrayed
God's wonders, so magnificently displayed!

Just as these lights meet halfway everyday
God will do the same for you today
Open your heart and let his light in to shine
Filling your heart with a love that is unconditional and divine!

Eternal light can be yours forevermore
Just knock and ask him to open his door
With open arms, he awaits to welcome you
He is always there for you to come to!

I am the light of the world, the Lord Jesus said
Eternal life awaits through him and just lays ahead
God the Father created light for us to live in
His Son, Jesus is the light to save us from sin!

Lights from heaven, sent to us full of love
From our Mighty Lord in heaven above
Awesome and wondrous is the Lord's light
Living in it, divine light will shine forever in our sight!

Love The Little Children

All children are precious in the Lord's eyes
He hears every sound from them, even their cries
His love for them is abounding and pure
Little children, Jesus truly adores!

Let the little children come to me the Lord said
For my love for them can never be misread
Small and innocent, they are to me
Children of my flock, they always will be!

Cloth and feed them, the responsibility is yours
A child is a blessing, not something to ignore
Remember, as small as they may be
Like you, one day I want them to come home with me!

Guide and teach them my loving ways
When raised with love in their hearts, forever, it stays
Teach them my commandments to obey
Living by my words, you must convey!

Show them compassion, as I have unto you
Wipe their tears away, be the shoulder they lean unto
Give them praise for the good things they do
And their love for you, will shine through!

Explain to them exactly what faith in me is all about
They will be wondering, without any doubt
Tell them that loving the Lord is first and foremost
Love him and to you, he will stay close!

Place hope in their hearts, for it does a lot of things
A brighter tomorrow is one thing it brings
Teach them to love one another like sister and brother
You are their parents, they will have no other!

Blessed are the little children whom Jesus loves and adores
All a blessing from heaven, who could ask for anything more?
Love them and teach them, never to depart
For your Lord's love is embedded deep within your heart!

We Are Christians By Our Love

And they will know we are Christians by our love, we sing
Now and forevermore to Jesus, Our Mighty King!
The Lord's love shines on those who worship him, in heaven above
He will keep us surrounded in his endless love!
Everyday, we will walk with him hand in hand
Yes, united in his his love, we will walk throughout the land!
We will speak to others about his word
It's not right to hide, what we've heard!
Love one another, he commands
Let love be seen in your actions, he demands!
Know that your Saviour Jesus loves you
Now and forever, he is there to turn to!
Open your mouths, sing out loud
Willingly, stand up for your Lord, tall and proud!
We will be kind to all others and not bold
Everyone needs compassion, that we've been told!
And they'll know we are Christians by our love, we sing
Really, we love Our Lord Jesus, he's Our King!
Everyday we will worship and give him praise
Constantly, abiding in Our Lord's loving ways!
Helping all those who are in need, when we can
Remember, giving is all part of God's great plan!
In every way possible, we will symbolize a white dove
Showing and speaking of Our Lord's Love!
Trusting and giving our lives only to Our Lord Jesus
Is that not what he truly expects of us!
Amazing is everything about Our Lord Jesus, that we can think of

Never-ending and and endless is His Love!
Smiling at all and each other as we go
Brings joy unto the heart and it glows!
Yesterday is gone and tomorrow is in sight
One by one, we must try and make all sinners see His light!
Upon each loving step that we take
Really, another child of Our Lord becomes awake!
Love the Lord with all your heart, soul and mind
Obey the Lord's words, and love all mankind!
Walking only with love in your heart
Visible to all that you are a Christian,
Everlasting love from Our Lord Jesus,will never depart.

Precious Lord (A Prayer)

Precious Lord, humbly I come to you in prayer
There is no other love like yours, that can compare
Gently walking beside me day to day
Always, in my heart, your love will stay.

Precious Lord, how I love you so
And far from you, I will never go
I stand before you, humble and meek
All of my life,day after day, week after week.

Precious Lord, My Savior and King
In praise to you, my soul will sing
Creator of life and all I see
Forever, let me walk along, with thee.

Precious Lord, the Almighty One
Your love is so great, you sent Jesus, your only Son
To save us all from eternal death
How badly he suffered, before taking his final breath.

Precious Lord, please set my soul free
Wash away my burdens and sins from me
Let my spirit be free like the birds up in the sky
Promise always to stay near me and close by.

Linda Laybolt
Whispers From Heaven

Precious Lord, My Most Trusting, Dearest Friend
Please stay with me, to the very end
Hold your arms open for me to come into
Then, gently carry me home Lord, to be with you.

Seeking Love

I heard you say you wished you had someone to love and love you
That you wanted someone to be faithful and true
That you are tired of playing the waiting game
I am here but I have never heard you once call my name!

You say have have no one in your life whom you can trust
That in a relationship, it is a must
You want a trust-worthly person for your life to share
I am here and I truly do care!

You say you need someone to share your dreams and hopes with
You don't need a life full of riddles and myths
You want someone to believe in you and you in them
I am here and I am him!

You say you want someone to put your beliefs in
To make your heart feel love, outside and in
You want to be filled with happiness and not sorrow
I am here with a brighter tomorrow!

You say you just want someone to care
The thoughts of being alone, you can no longer bare
You need someone to talk and to listen
I am here with all of my wisdom!

You say you seek comfort and compassion
Attention and affection
A shoulder to lean on and confide into
I am here, I am always here for and with you!

Linda Laybolt
Whispers From Heaven

I am here and have been since the beginning of time
I would never abandon you as you are mine
You are my child and I love you so
I think the time has come for us to say hello!

Everything you seek or long for, I can offer to thee
All you have to do is place your love, trust and faith in me
I am the Lord, your Father who reigns in heaven above
And you, my dear child will always have my love!

Angels From Heaven

I see the lonely souls walk by
I can see the sadness in their eyes
Little do they know, where ever they go
I can see an angel walking behind them slow.
Sometimes I can see more than one
Sent from Heaven by Gods only Son.
Silently and discreetly following them everyday
Protecting them in every possible way.
Most people do not even realize they are there
But angels on earth are seen everywhere.
For every person that has been blessed with birth
An angel from Heaven is sent to earth.
I can see the love they have for you all the time
I know for a fact, they are truly divine.
I can see everything from up here in Heaven above
Because I sent them to you, full of my everlasting love!
Angels are one of Gods most precious gifts sent to you
They will forever stay beside you to see you through.

Standing In Line At Heavens Gates

High in the Heavens Above
Sits immense mansions, full of love.
Surrounded by huge Pearly Gates
Inside Jesus, My Lord and Saviour awaits!

Not just anyone can enter inside
Many are left standing lost, on the outside.
Only Jesus holds the key to enter within
You have to know Him personally, to get in.

Standing on the outside, looking in
It's too late now to repent of any sin.
If only does not exist here
Thoughts of never getting in would be hard to bare!

Inside you see many of your loved ones, waving to you
Many of your friends are also in full view.
You can see the radiance of love in their eyes shine
Only happiness exists here, everything here is beyond fine!

Even standing on the ouside, everything looks so grand
This trully indeed is the Promised Land!
Inside you see many huge mansions, that seem to never end
As you keep looking about, for that very special friend.

The streets really are paved with gold
Just like it was written, in the Bible foretold.
You can hear the angels voices singing from within
The angelic orchestra never stops playing, to start over again.

It looks like gardens upon garden everywhere to be seen
With radiant colours, it is quite the masterpiece picture scene.
But then again, it was created by the Master, My Creator
Nothing exists on earth or in the heavens, that is greater!

Standing in line at Heavens Gates, looking all around
Watching and listening, without making a sound.
At last, I see My Lord Jesus, I am standing in front of the Gate
He smiles and says Come in My Child, you no longer have to wait!

His Abounding Love

Cease the moments, of today and everyday
Maybe, good things will come your way.
Give your family, an extra hug or two
Always say the words, I love you.
Smile at someone, you don't know
Perhaps, they might be feeling low.
Pick up the phone, call an old friend
Endlessly talk and laugh, without end.
Be kind to others, that surround you
You have not walked, in their shoes.
Help an elderly person to cross the street
Or give a homeless person, something to eat.
Spend some time, with a sick friend today
Let them know you care, in a big way.
Help the little child, that fell off her bike
Surely, you remember, what that felt like.
Feed a stray, that lands at your door
Abandon animals will love you, forevermore.
Donate your old clothes, that you no longer wear
Definitely, someone could use them, out there.
Go for a walk in the park, find a bench for you to sit
Enjoy Gods beauty that surrounds you, bit by bit.
Then today give thanks to your Lord, In Heaven Above
Who has filled your heart, With His abounding Love!

Linda Laybolt
Whispers From Heaven

Whispers Of The Heart

Remain Still, Humbly Listen to the Whispers Of God
Softly speaking to your heart, for you to hear
Reaching out to you, Full of Comfort and Compassion
The Lord is A Loving God, Forever Closeby and Near!

Exalt yourself, in the Refuge of His Realms
Be Grateful to Him for Shielding you, under His Wing
Fear Not your Burdens, for they are Now His
His arms are open wide, to take hold of and cling!

Partake the Belief and Glory, of His Mighty Strength
Graciously Give Thanks, as He unfolds it unto you
Seek the Lord and His Strength, Seek His presence
The Lord Blesses those when it is Him, they turn to!

Follow The Lord, Let Him Be Your Guide to Lead The Way
Open your eyes, from the Depths of Darkness Within
His Light Never Dims or Fades, It Remains Forever Lit
He is The Light Of The World, and Always has been!

Place all your Faith, Trust and Hope in the Lord
Be Embraced With His Love, No Greater Love you will ever find
The Lords Love For You is Eternal, Everlasting to Everlasting
Love the Lord With all your Heart, Soul, Strength and Mind.

Since the beginning of time, God has spoken to His People
He is Holy, Loving, Righteous, Powerful, PURE, REAL and MIGHTY
Whispers Of The Heart from Your Loving Father, In Heaven
The Lord God Almighty, who lives For All Eternity!

Eternal Life Awaits

Lord she cried out in anguish, What wrong have I done?
Am I not, one of your loved ones?
Why have you placed this incurable disease upon me?
I'm just barely twenty, how can this be?

I want to live a long life, get married and grow old
I want to have children of my own, to love and hold
I have so many things in life, that I want to do
Dreams in my heart, that I long to pursue!

But now that has been all taken away, by you
Healthy as can be, then sick and dying, out of the blue
What kind of God does this, the answers I need to know
Where is the love for your children, Where did it go?

As she knelt down on her hands and knees, she bowed her head
Tears rolled from eyes, regretting the words she had said
I am sorry Lord for being so selfish and unkind
But I somehow feel forgotten, alone and left behind!

Lord, I am so full of fear of what is, to take place
I need you to Comfort me, I need Your Loving Embrace
As she knelt, she could feel His Presence surround her
The Warmth of Everlasting Love, from her Heavenly Father!

All the anguish and fear, she had felt was gone
Now Safe in the Refuge of her Lord, life would go on
Peace and contentment filled her soul, with His Love
Eternal Life Awaits, With Her Lord in Heaven Above!

Within Your Love

I know your eyes are upon me
From you, I cannot hide or flee!
Silently watching every move I make
Walking beside me, every step I take!
I am never alone and on my own
Your seed of love has been sown!
I feel your presence everywhere
I have comfort, knowing you are there!
Just because I cannot see you
Doesn't mean, you are not real and true!
Trust and faith, go hand in hand
That very few can understand!
Just like the days of the long ago past
People still have doubts, questions are asked!
The scientists try to discredit you
With all their different points of view!
No matter what they say and do
My love for you shines through and through!
You have blessed me in so many ways
Within your reach, I will stay always!
Your Unconditional Divine Love touches my soul
My heart and spirit are one, now whole!
My Heavenly Father, My Lord, My God, in Heaven Above
Forever, I want to stay embraced "Within your Love!"

The Trumpets

I hear the trumpets, gently floating through the sky
Armies of angels, can be seen, way up high!
The Lamb of My God, is On His way
Get on your knees, for it is " The Lords Day!"
I hear the trumpets, as they move from sea to sea

Linda Laybolt
Whispers From Heaven

I hear the trumpets, playing peacefully to me!
I hear the angels sing to all, We Proclaim
Blessed is Our Lord, Holy is His Name!
I hear the trumpets, as they soar across the sky
I hear the music, as it plays from way up high!
I hear the angels, Sing Out With Love,
This is Your Lord, from Heaven Above!
I hear them sing out Hallelujah!
Hallelujah! to Our Dear Lord!
I hear the trumpets, as they float across the sky
Armies of Angels can be seen, way up high!
I see My Saviour! My Lord, My King!
All Praise and Glory, Be given unto Him!
I see the white doves, flying in the air
Singing with the angels, The Lord Is Here!
The trumpets are sounding, the music plays
That My Lord Jesus, is here to stay!
Hallelujah! The King Is Here!
Hallelujah! Hallelujah! Hallelujah!

I Was There

I saw the tears fall from your eyes as you cried today
Gently, I rushed to your side and wiped them away
I watched you trip and fall to the ground
Gently, I picked you up without making a sound
I heard you say, I'm lonely and blue
Gently, I placed my loving arms around you
I knew it was you, when you cried out in pain
Gently , I rushed to your side once more again.
I listened as you wept that you were on your own
Gently, I held you close, you are never alone.
I heard you that night softly pray on your knees to me
Gently, I kissed your forehead goodnight, setting your soul free!

Going Home

The voice softly said, follow the light
Out of the darkness, it appeared so bright.
Just follow me, I'll take you there
But I would not move, to go anywhere.

Where was I? What was going on?
Who was this woman trying to persuade me, to tag along?
I looked all around, darkness surrounded me
Except for the glowing light, how could this be?

This has to be the strangest dream, I have ever had
When it is over, I'll really be glad!
The woman approached me again
One would almost think, she was a long lost friend.

Wake up! Wake up! I silently cried!
Wishing I had a place to run and hide.
However, when I looked this time at her, all fear was gone
I knew exactly what was going on!

Hand in hand towards the Light, the two of us went
She was my Guardian Angel, that Heaven had sent!
In the blink of an eye, I was in Heaven Above
At Home with My Father, surrounded by everlasting love!

Blessings

May God Bless you, each and every day
And send many Blessings to you today.
May the Lord God in Heaven Above
Fill your heart, with His everlasting Love.

Whispers From Heaven

Let peace and comfort, fill your soul
Let their be joy & laughter to from the young to the old.
Don't let too many tears, fall from your eyes
Don't let disappointment, give you too many sighs.

Try and make the most of your day
Remember God is with you, every step of the way.
And if sad times should befall upon you
God will give you comfort, He sees everything too.

No matter how rough, your day may be
It won't last forever, Jesus says "Come to me."
Be grateful and thankful for each and everyday
For without the Lords Blessings, you wouldn't be here today!

Let's Cross The Bridge

Let's cross the bridge together, you and I
And we'll watch for white doves to fly by
We'll listen real hard, to hear them sing
With the angels, to Our Mighty King!

Rainbows stretch across the blue sky
So many vivid colors that meet the eye
Gardens of flowers can be seen everywhere
No beauty on earth could ever compare.

If there is this much beauty on the outside
Imagine what it is like, on the inside!
The closer we get, the more we see
I wonder if this is the way, it was meant to be!

The sounds of music echo through the air
Angelic voices can be heard everywhere
What a wondrous place this is going to be
Not just for you but also me!

Linda Laybolt
Whispers From Heaven

Look over there, finally I see big Pearly Gates
My heart says inside, My Saviour awaits!
C'mon don't be shy, let's go in
A new life for us is about to begin!

The Dove

I wish I was a bird flying in the sky
I'd fly away to lands, way up high!
I would like to be a white dove
Endlessly, spreading peace and love!

I'd have no worries at all to think of
Just flying free, in the skies above!
Now and again, I'd stop in a tree
For a rest and to see who needs me!

I would go from town to town
Spread my love to all around!
Beauty may be mine to behold
But Love is mine, from days of old!

I would look for those with sorrow
Give them hopes of a better tomorrow!
A little bit of love here and there
Soon gets to be felt everywhere!

I would bring many smiles to faces
As I would fly to lots of places!
I would put warmth in a heart
Instill love that would never depart!

I'd sing praise and glory to God Above
After all, I am a dove!
Sent from the Heaven's Above
To fill the world with God's Love!

I Am Always Here To Come To

I heard a whisper in my ear
Softly calling my name
I looked around but could not see
From where exactly, it came!
So I sort of shrugged it away
But then I heard it once more
Again, I looked but no one was there
Just as it happened before!
Then I heard a voice say to me
You are not alone, I am here!
I suddenly felt warm all over
I did not want this feeling to disappear!
I knew in my heart that it was The Lord
Once again, He had come to my rescue
I had poured my out heart to Him in tears
Since He always knows what to do!
I could feel the strength of His arms
As they gently wrapped around me
I could feel His Compassion and Comfort
My burdens were now gone and free!
But most of all, I could feel His Love
Surrounding me from Heaven
I had sinned and I felt so ashamed
But I knew now, that all had been forgiven!
I bowed my head and said a prayer
Lord, temptation is so very strong
Please stay with me and guide me
So I will do right, not wrong!
I can't make it alone, without you
I am so sorry for straying away
Please be my light, when darkness falls
Each and every day!

Then, I heard a soft voice whisper
My Child, I am always here with you
My Love for you is Endless
I Am Always Here To Come To!

The Greatness Of Heaven

Imagine living in a world without sin
Imagine having a feeling of peace, deep within!
Imagine a world living under one ruler, one nation
Imagine a world without evil temptation!
Imagine a world where no hunger exists
Imagine a world with no excuses, no buts or ifs!
Imagine a world with no pain or sorrow
Imagine a world where there is always tomorrow!
Imagine a world where darkness is of the past
Imagine a world full of divine light everlast!
Imagine a world with no fighting or wars
Imagine a world where only love outpours!
Imagine a world where only beauty is all around
Imagine no greater place than this, is to be found!
Imagine a world with no tears or silent cries
Imagine a world where there are no good-byes!
Imagine a world where there is no rich or poor
Imagine a world all are equal forevermore!
Imagine a world where there is no shame or blame
Imagine a world living under one family name!
Imagine a world where everyone is sister and brother
Imagine a world where everyone Loves One Another!
Imagine being in The Great Kingdom Of Heaven Above
Imagine being surrounded by God's Divine Love!
Imagine being with angels, and with them you'll sing
Imagine Giving All Praise and Glory, to Our Mighty King!
Imagine being in Heaven, full of bliss and peace
Imagine knowing that, Never it will cease!
Imagine being with Our Lord Jesus, and God The Father, The Almighty
Imagine Forever Living Here In Heaven, For All Eternity!

All Praise and All Glory Be Given To God The Father, who has promised us all these things through His Loving Son Jesus, "Lord Of Lords, King Of Kings!" Forever And Ever!

Love The Lord With All Your Heart

I believe in God the Father, the Almighty in Heaven Above
I believe in My Lord Jesus, who reigns in the Glory of Love!
I believe in the Holy Spirit, through Him all God's Love does shine
I believe that the Holy Bible is the True Word Of God, Completely Divine!

Stand tall and proud within the Light of God, Now and Always
Holy is the Lord God Almighty, Righteous are His Divine Ways!
Let the Warmth of His Love, completely surround you
Humbly, Rejoice Giving Him All Praise and All Glory, in all you say and do!

Blessed are the Meek and the Humble, who Love the Lord each day
The Kingdom of God will be theirs to Behold, never to be taken away!
Love the Lord with all your Heart, Soul, Strength and Mind
When He looks in your heart, Love is what you want Him to find!

Love the Lord, Your God above everything, Always place Him First above all
Nothing can compare to the Blessings of God, upon you as they fall!
God so loved the world that He sent His Son Jesus, to conquer sin
Eternal Life can be found Only, by those who believe in Him!

Walk with the Lord's Love in your heart, radiating it to all you see
Be Kind, Compassionate, and Loving, just as the Lord would be!
Forgive others if they do you wrong, Do No Harm unto others
Jesus preached in The Vine and The Branches, "To Love One Another!"

Linda Laybolt
Whispers From Heaven

Live a Life of Love, A Life Full of God's Divine Love
Placing All of Your Faith, Trust And Hope in God in Heaven Above!
My God Is Love, Alpha and Omega, What Was, What Is, and What Is To Be
FOREVER LIVES FOR ALL ETERNITY!

In My Hour Of Need

In my hour of need, I call upon you
To come to my rescue, to see me through!
When my whole world is falling apart
Only you can see, what's really in my heart!

No one else could ever feel the hurt inside
Or see the silent tears, I've cried!
Always, I keep coming to you again and again
For only you, can stop the pouring rain!

I can take all my troubles to you anytime
When I see a mountain that looks, hard to climb!
I feel your presence surround me, when I pray
When I ask you to take my burdens, you never turn away!

When I say, Lord I need a shoulder to lean on
Your loving arms reach out, to rest my head upon!
When I cannot see for the darkness has blocked my sight
Your candle glows, giving rays of light!

Your divine love gives me strength, making me strong
To face the many battles of life, that I may transpire upon!
I have complete peace of mind, knowing you are there
I can come anytime to you, with my problems to share!

Compassion and comfort, await for me in prayer
Anytime, any place, "Your Divine Love is Everywhere!"
My Lord in Heaven, You will always be the one I turn to
My Loving Father, you hold all answers and know what to do!

The Covenant In The Sky

High up in the sky, a rainbow stretches far and wide
Beautiful arrays of colors, side by side!
Nestled in the clouds, shaped like a bow
Appearing only after a rain, the exquisite rainbow!
The rainbow has been around, for a very long time
Placed in the sky by God Himself, it is certainly divine!
After the great flood, where it rained for forty days and nights
Noah was told to come out of the ark, the time was right!
God blessed Noah and his family, for obeying His commands
Giving Noah and his family, complete reign of the lands!
Noah had saved two of every living animal, on earth
God had given to mankind, a second chance, a new rebirth!
So after God had blessed Noah, He made a covenant forevermore
Placing a rainbow in the clouds, to remind Him of life before!
God said, when it appears and I look down and see it
I will remember my covenant which I have made, and not forget!
Never again will the waters become a flood to destroy, all life here
The rainbow is the sign of my everlasting covenant, and will not disappear!
A covenant established by God to all life on earth, of every kind
Sealed in the clouds, the beautiful rainbow is the bind!
Next time you gaze in wonder at a rainbow, stretched across the sky
God could be looking at it too, remembering His covenant from way up high!

In God's Loving Trust

We all return to the ground, from which we were created
As the saying goes, "Ashes to Ashes, Dust to Dust!"
However, this does not mean that this is the end
Eternal life awaits for all who believe, "In God's Loving Trust!"

Linda Laybolt
Whispers From Heaven

What exactly is this word we call trust, we may ask
The dictionary defines it as having faith or believing in
An example is God, Our Creator, not surprising at all
He has been there since the beginning, and always has been!
In God's Loving Trust, a ray of light shines on me
Forever, in your grace, is where I want to be!
In God's Loving Trust, comfort and compassion I find
For only you Lord, gives me peace of mind!
In God's Loving Trust, unconditional love is there to behold
Refuge is mine as loving arms reach out, to take ahold!
In God's Loving Trust, My Loving Lord awaits
For His Child to come Home, behind the Golden Gates!
God has been true to us, right from the very start
So why from Him, would we ever want to part?
Trust is to have faith, faith is to believe, beyond all doubt
Forever, I will remain,"In God's Loving Trust", day in and day out!

A Prayer For All Prayers

A Prayer for all Prayers
For you Lord to embrace
A Prayer for all Prayers
All heading to one Holy Place!

A Prayer for all Prayers
I'm sending to you Lord, today
A Prayer for all Prayers
One small prayer is on its way!

A Prayer for all Prayers
From everywhere here, Lord to you
A Prayer for all Prayers
One small prayer, for you to listen to!

A Prayers for all Prayers
To give comfort to those in despair
A Prayer for all Prayers
For those who come to you in prayer!

A Prayer for all Prayers
Is on its way up to you
A Prayer for all Prayers
For only you Lord, know what to do!

A Prayer for all Prayers
To You, My Lord!

Never Stop Praying

So many problems, so many people uncertain about the future
So many rocks and boulders, await on that hill!
The journey may be long and very tiresome
Take comfort knowing, the Lord is beside you still!
Heartbreak and sorrow may follow you, these days
You ponder and may continually ask "Lord, Why Me?"
Am I being punished for something of the past, I have done?
Why has this happened? How can this be?
You struggle back and forth in your mind
Continually questioning, the path that has come your way
No answers seem to come in sight, which ever way you turn
You may even wonder, God let this happen, so why should I pray?
The hills we climb in life are stages, we all go through
Some hills continue on to others, while some may not
If we happen to be on our last hill of life, as we know it
Are we going to turn our back on all, that we have been taught?
Now is the time, we need Our Father in Heaven, even more
Now is the time to think of the promised future, that awaits
It may be an end to this life on earth, as we know it
But a better life awaits for us, beyond those Pearly Gates!
Our Lord Jesus suffered in pain and despair
Not once did he turn away from, His Father Above
Instead he continually prayed through it all, on the cross
Never losing His Faith, His Trust and His Love!

Linda Laybolt
Whispers From Heaven

With Jesus beside us, every step of the way
We should have no fears about, what tomorrow may be
Love the Lord with all your heart, soul, mind and strength
The Kingdom of Heaven is for Eternity!

Blessings From Heaven

I feel you watching me
In every move I make or do
Knowing you are there
Brings me closer to you!

When I feel lonely and blue
Thats when I feel you most
It's those times I feel your comfort
As you draw me close!

When I am in pain and suffering
Compassion is given unto me
Comforting my hurt that I feel inside
Releasing it, to set it free!

When my mind feels lost
Debating about which path to take
Your guidance is always there
In what choices, I make!

When I feel unloved and unwanted
You come willingly to my rescue
With your divine unconditional Love
You always know what to do!

When I just want to talk
And no one is there but you and I
I talk casually to you about everything
You are my best friend, always on stand by!

Linda Laybolt
Whispers From Heaven

When I am happy, things are going good
I sense content in all that I do
I remember to give thanks to you, My Lord
As I know these Blessings are from you!

High up in the Heavens above
All worship you My Lord, With Love
Praise and Glory will always be yours
My Lord, My Friend whom I Love and Adore!

We Are Never Alone

It is the middle of the night
And all is not right with me
I have this new unknown feeling
Going all through me, what can it possibly be?

I try to reach for the light by my bed
But am unable to do so, as I am too weak
As I yell for help to come to my side
I realize no words do I hear, for I cannot speak.

Laying there helpless, I could hardly move
I knew my days on earth had finally come to an end
Alone and forsaken by all my family
I moaned and sighed, wishing I had a friend.

Darkness completely surrounds me,
I feel scared about death for the first time ever
I never really thought much about it
I guess everyone thinks, they're gonna live forever!

I decided I better say a little prayer
To My Lord Jesus in Heaven Above
I guess my time is drawing near to an end
Thank you Lord for all you have given me, especially your love.

Linda Laybolt
Whispers From Heaven

Thank you Lord for walking down every path with me
Thank you for wiping away the many tears
Thank you for never forsaking me or abandoning me
Thank you for carrying me so many times, through the years.

All of a sudden, I see a glowing light
Someone has finally come to my rescue
The light gets brighter and brighter
Am I seeing things, Lord Jesus, is that really you?

As I look up and see the smile on His face
I feel the warmth as He holds me in His Loving Embrace.
I am not alone and forsaken, what was I ever thinking of?
My Lord Jesus has always been here, full of everlasting Love!

My Thoughts Fo Today

There is always some conflict
in this world that we live in.
If it s not war or genocide,
along with the natural disasters
that happen along the way.
Makes one wonder.......
Why there has to be so much
conflict in the world today.
Are not enough people killed
from all the disasters that we have
along with the accidents
and killings that occur everyday
So what happened to
Thou Shalt Not Kill?
Is it right for one to erase
people with a different
ethnic belief or way of life?
Jus because you do not like them?
In the Bible there were
allsorts of wars and genocides
Because God had only one nation

Linda Laybolt
Whispers From Heaven

that He favored above all.
Because they had faith and believed
In God Only!
Then why were all these different
people and nations created.
For s it not God who gave
life to every living thing on
this earth, and in the seas and shies up above.
Yet wars and genocides have been
with us since the beginning of time,
according to the Old Testament in the Bible.
Yet God sent His Only Son
to this earth; to dwell and preach among us.
For a period of time
He converted many Gentiles to Christianity.
Are not two of Gods Commandments
Thou shalt not kill and
Love thy neighbour as thy self?
Yet politicians are quick to judge
and send us to war
for us and our kids
to kill or be killed.
By calling it a peacekeeping force
or police action.
Are we not all the same
in Gods yes?
We all believe in something and someone.
As long as this world is going to survive.
There always be wars ad conflict
somewhere in the world!
So where is the love
for your common man?
Do we not realize
that love is he greatest
commandment of all.
Therefore cannot we
be more understanding of each other,
instead of condemning one another.
Therefore look at the beam in your eye,

Linda Laybolt
Whispers From Heaven

before condemning one with
just a slinter in his eye.
Now let the love of Jesus
Be with you all,
Now and for Always.

By John

As He Looks Down From His Throne

When we are happy to see the dawn of a new day
And we smile as the sun rises into the sky
I wonder if the Lord is smiling too
As He looks down from His Throne, from way up high.

When the little birds echo sweet lullabies to our ears
And we listen to the the different songs that they sing
I wonder if the Lord is listening too
As He looks down from His Throne, & the happiness they bring.

When a blooming flower catches our eye
And we cannot stop gazing at its beauty and splendor
I wonder if the Lord is full of admiration too
As He looks down from His Throne, knowing He was its Creator.

When a colorful rainbow stretches across the sky
And we amazingly adore it, the colors each in a perfect line
I wonder if the Lord is watching too
As He looks down fron His Throne, knowing it is truly divine.

When a heart is full of compassion and love
Everything around you becomes visible, to your sight
I don't have to wonder if the Lord sees this too
I know He is looking down from His Throne, at you in pure delight!

Linda Laybolt
Whispers From Heaven

Have A Blessed Day!

Live your dreams to the fullest
Don't settle for second best
Live a life that's full of laughter
Try not to get over-stressed.

Be kind to all around you
Show compassion to those in need
Lend a helping hand, when you can
Don't lead a life, full of greed.

Don't be judgmental of other people
You have not walked in their shoes
Some day you may be down and out
Or suffering with a bad case of the blues.

When you are alone and bored
Sing out the words of your favorite song
Even if you are way out of tune
If it makes you happy, it can't be wrong.

Be sure to keep in touch with your friends
Old or new, it's good to reminisce
Don't be lonely and hide in solitude
Friends can really put you in a high state of bliss.

Enjoy the little things in your life
Get out of the house, go to a park
Sit back and watch the children as they play
Why sit at home and be in the dark?

Always keep family close to your heart
Tell them you love them whenever you can
Don't live to regret harsh words that you said
No one wants to wind up a lonely old woman or man.

Linda Laybolt
Whispers From Heaven

And with each new day that comes your way
Give thanks to the Lord in Heaven Above
We never know what each day will bring
But one thing is certain, we can "Always Count On GOD'S LOVE!"

A Home Called Earth

Isaiah 45:18 For this is what the LORD says-- he who created the heavens, he is God; he who fashioned and made the earth, he founded it; he did not create it to be empty, but formed it to be inhabited-- he says: "I am the LORD, and there is no other.

I gave it all to you because I love you
You are My children, you always have been
From the beginning of time, I had plans for you
You are Mine, you are My Beloved kin.

Just because thousands of years have passed by
Does not change the facts at all, for I Am The Lord
The scientists think they know it all with their theories
But when it comes to me as Creator, I am completely ignored!

In the beginning, God created the heavens and the earth
With love in my heart, I made a home for you from the earth
I gave you all you need to survive, and much, much more
From the dust of the ground, I gave Adam and Eve birth.

Without all of this being done by me, you would not exist
I am God...I am The Lord....there is no other but me
Yet centuries go by and still you question my existence
I Am Your Creator....All that ever Was, Is and Yet To Be!

Take a good look at all the beauty that surrounds you
From the the mountains and trees, to the fish in the seas
The animals that walk amongst you, the flowers that bloom
The warmth of the sun as it shines; the soft summer breeze.

Linda Laybolt
Whispers From Heaven

Never-ending elegance, glamour and uniqueness
My beauty is everywhere, dazzling within your sight
Everything is within your grasp, for I Am The Lord
Everything I created for you is Perfect and Right!

There is so much beauty on earth for you to behold
The earth is your home; a gift to you, from me
Take care of your Home, as you would your son or daughter
I made it not to be empty but for my children to walk free.

New Living Translation (©2007)
"I am the Alpha and the Omega--the beginning and the end," says the Lord God. "I am the one who is, who always was, and who is still to come--the Almighty One."

Every Step Of The Way

There once was a girl, full of dreams
But none were to be, so it seems.
Trials and tribulations were her companion, you see
No place to hide, never being set free.

Each day at the dawn of a new day
She wondered what lies ahead today?
Will it be smooth sailing for a change
Or will she be still bound to her chains?

Whatever would happen, she knew she'd get through
Because the Lord was always there, to turn to.
Just about everyday, she'd ask the same thing
Lord get me through today, tucked under your wing!

There were days that never seemed to end
But there were good days that laid around the bend.
The trials and tribulations, never seemed to cease
And her mind was never really at peace.

Linda Laybolt
Whispers From Heaven

She often wondered, what she had done so very wrong
For these hardships to follow, her all lifelong.
Then, one day she said to herself, "Life isn't all that bad"
And started to count all the blessings she had.

She realized that her life was just the way, it was meant to be
Even though it took a lifetime, for her to see.
The Lord had been with her, every step of the way
He never once turned His back on her, and walked away.

For in every hour of deepest darkness, she saw a light
Shining off in a distance, within her sight.
She always knew that things would someday change
And He would free her, from the bounded chains.

Trials and tribulations still follow her today
But now her mind is full of peace, everything will be ok.
They say, The Lord works in mysterious ways
Always remember He is beside you, every step of the way!

I Am A Child Of God

I am a Child of God
When I was born, I was baptized on that day
I was born from Abraham's Seed
My family goes back in time; a long, long way.

I am a Child of God
My Father is the Creator of everything, that you see
Believe it or not, nothing would exist without Him
My Father; "What Was, Is and Yet To Be".....

I am a Child of God
The Great Alpha and Omega, The Great Almighty
The Great Protector of All His Children
My Father parted the Big Red Sea.

Linda Laybolt
Whispers From Heaven

I am a Child of God
My Father is Holy, Righteous and Pure
Merciful, Forgiving and Caring
Being His Child, I feel Safe and Secure.

I am a Child of God
My Father is Loving and Kind
Unfailable and Trustworthy to all His Children
No greater Love will I ever find.

I am a Child of God
My Father is Real and so Full of Love
The truth is "My Father is Perfect"
My Father, Divine Master of All & Heaven Above!

I am a Child of God
I feel so happy, knowing that He is My Father
My Father is the Supreme Power of All
Blessed are the Sons and Daughters, who Love Our Father!

Spring

Waves of warmth fall to the ground from the suns rays
Spring has finally appeared, these past few days.
Everywhere flowers emerge to the surface of the ground
Blooming in all colors, without making a sound.

Little voices echo with their songs, throughout the air
Birds gather together making their nests, with great care.
Pussy willows arise to the occasion, waiting for me on the trees
As they sway softly back and forth, to the gentle breeze.

Leaves and buds are appearing on the rose bushes everywhere
Soon their sweet smell will dominate throughout the air.
Daffodils, blue bells, hyancinthus and crocus are in full bloom
Tulips spread throughout the yard, taking up so much room.

When God created the seasons, He gave us so much to see
Each season falls in place, in perfect harmony.
Just as a season dies, a new one is about to arise
Full of beauty and wonder, right before our eyes.

So enjoy the awesome beauty of the seasons, especially spring
Spring is the season of life, a renewal of everything.
It was all created for you and I to enjoy, Out Of Love
By The Master Himself, Our Heavenly Father; In Heaven Above.

Divine Light

Divine Light, of Gods Loving Grace
Forever keep us, within your embrace
Shine on us, every step of the way
Even when we tend to stray away.

Divine Light, of Our Most Holy Lord
Forever by all, be deeply adored
Surround your children with your light
Keeping us always, within your sight.

Divine Light, of Gods Loving Strength
Forever keep us, within arms length
Shield us from any harm that comes our way
Morning, noon, night and day.

Divine Light, Full of Gods Great Wisdom
Forever keep us on the path to Your Kingdom
Forgive us of all my earthly wrongs and sins
Let Heaven be where our new life begins.

Divine Light, Holy, Infinite and Supreme
Forever be there on us to gleam
Divine Light, Full of Gods Everlasting Love
Is the place we never want to let go of!

My Son, My Son, How I Love Thee!

I feel the pain
I feel the shame
As if I were there with you
If only, you knew.

I hurt inside
Many tears, I've cried
The memory won't go away
In my heart, it'll always stay.

I hear the angels weep around me
Sorrow is all mine eyes can see
How could they hurt you so?
This no one will ever know.

No man is without sin
Only you, from your soul within
Perfect in every possible way
Yet, scorned, beaten and taken away.

Guilty so they scream and shout
Tossed, turned and thrown about
The thorns buried deep within your head
King of the Gentiles, the sign read.

Endlessly, you suffered for all of us
My Loving Friend, My Beloved Son Jesus
Yet through it all, you never scorned them
You kept you faith, Son of God of Bethlehem.

You never stopped praying to your Father
You were the Chosen One, there is no other
Seeking forgiveness for those who had hurt you
Forgive them Father, "They know not what they do!"

Linda Laybolt
Whispers From Heaven

I heard you that day call my name
Ever since then, things will never be the same
My Beloved Son died on a cross for all mankind
No greater love than this will you ever find.

Without Jesus, no sins would be forgiven
Without Jesus, a chance at a new life would not been given
Jesus is the Way, the Light of the world for you
It's all up to you in all you say and do.

My Son Jesus willingly took the ultimate sacrifice
So that you would have eternal life, more than suffice
He holds the key to Heavens Gate to enter within
For you a new life awaits to begin.

Never again will My Son suffer at mans hands
For He shall be known as King of the Lands
A crown of Gold rests upon His Precious Head
King of Kings, Lord of Lords is what will be said.

Nations upon Nations will worship My Son
For Jesus, gave it all as the Chosen One
My Son, My Son, I could never forsake you
You are mine and perfect in all you do.

You think I did not grieve for you on the cross
I felt your pain that day, I felt the worlds loss
Tears fell endlessly from the angels eyes
Deep inside, I felt my silent cries.

But we had a plan to fulfill, My Son and I
Yet you still ask why Jesus had to die
To be raised from the dead, to set you all free
To one day live in Heaven, for all eternity.

My Son, My Son Jesus; How I Love Thee
Forever, you shall reign with me for all eternity
For together we are Alpha and Omega, What Was, Is and Yet To Be
From the beginning to the end of all eternity!

Life And Waters Path

Down the river to destinations unknown
The sun glistens upon the water as it flows
Our life is somewhat like the waters flowing downstream
We tend to follow it whatever path it goes.

From one second to the next, continually flowing
Never to return to the same spot again with time.
Comparing life to water, it leads the same path
You only pass by each second once, in a lifetime.

.Once that second is gone, it is considered the past
Time does not stand still for me or you
Just as the water never flows through the same spot again
That second in time, you cannot return to.

As I wander up to look down at a flowing water
The closer I get, the more I see my reflection
Just as the water continually flows, so does my life
My image moves like the water in many directions.

Live your life for today only as if its your last
Don't rely on tomorrow, the future is only seconds that may be
Place your love, faith and hope in the Lord, your God
Eternal life can be yours, like the water searches for the endless sea.

Water stands the test of time, only to return again
It evaporates to return in forms of rain, sleet or snow
Just as the water returns to its place of origin
The soul longs for its place of origin to go.

Without my Lord in my life, a state of confusion would rule within
There comes a time when you need something to reach out to
Never delay what you could have done yesterday
For the past is only a second away from you.

Linda Laybolt
Whispers From Heaven

The Lord is my Shepherd, he leadeth me beside still waters
There is no other place like this than with the Lord that exists
Don't let the waters keep flowing without direction through your life
Realize that second in time, what could have been, you've missed!

Our Meeting Place

There's a place in my heart where love comes shining through
Where I secretly go, just to be with you
A place of solitude, anytime I can retreat
It's the place where my Lord and I always meet.

We share all hopes, dreams and aspirations
Anything can be discussed, without any hesitations
A place just for us, a place of our own
A place where I go, so we can be alone.

A place where love is always for me to receive
Sometimes, I never want to leave
A place where compassion, is there for me to see
A place where he wipes my tears away for me.

A place for my prayers, no matter what they be
A secret place for my burdens and sins, for him to set free
A place full of love and so full of grace
A place where my Lord and I, lovingly embrace.

A place where I can give many thanks My Lord to
A place where I can sing joyfully to you
It's a place in my heart, where time stands still
A place for my soul, for his love to fill.

A place where light shines, making you never hard to find
A place anyone can have peace of mind
A place that is open to all, anytime night or day
A place where no one will ever get turned away.

Linda Laybolt
Whispers From Heaven

Divine is your love to all who come to you
Everlasting is your love to the sincere and true
You are there with open arms always
For it is your loving ways.

There's a place I will always go to be with you
A place in my heart that to you my soul opens to
There's a place that I go to meet with My Lord with love
And when I stop, I'll be at home with him in Heaven above

Battles Within The Heart

The world is yours, My Lord and so are we
Everything that ever was, is and yet to be
Creator of everything from sea to sea
You are My Lord, the Everlasting Almighty!

Sometimes I feel I am losing a battle inside of my heart
I get worried that your love for me will get torn apart
I don't know what I'd ever do, if I lost your love
Times like these, I need your loving arms to take hold of.

I try to obey your word as much as I possibly can
That is all part of your heavenly plan
Showing your love to all that I meet
Treating all with kindness and respect, and never to mistreat.

When I see all the sadness happening around me
I come in prayer most humbly unto thee
I know in my heart what is happening is wrong
But I need your love to keep me moving along.

Life is never a bed of roses, this everyone knows
But sometimes, the worst just grows and grows
When you are there standing there at my side
Your divine love helps me take it all in stride.

Linda Laybolt
Whispers From Heaven

Compassion is something that we all seek
For all the times we feel lost and weak
Not knowing which way is the right way to turn
Your words of comfort, is what we all yearn.

My love for you is embedded in my heart
My loving Lord, I hope nothing ever tears it apart
That's why I am asking you today
To never depart and go away.

There's a loving place that I always can go to
A place to take my burdens when I feel blue
A place that listens any time, day or night
Forever, My Loving Father is there shining his light!

Jesus And His Disciples

Come follow me and walk with me
Fishers of men, I want you to be
My Father says the time has is right
For all who love him to unite.

I will take you with me through the land
We will walk together hand in hand
You will be two of twelve disciples whom I love
Teaching my Father's Holy Words from heaven above.

We will journey from one place to another
We will teach the people to love each other
My Father says love is the only way
Faithfully trusting him, I will obey.

Walking with love in our hearts, so all will see
My Father's Kingdom is the place to be
Peace and harmony is there for all
My Father's mercy unto the righteous will fall.

Linda Laybolt
Whispers From Heaven

The days will be long, my Father has so much to be done
That's why I need you to follow me, one by one
For I have chosen you to teach my Father's Word
With my loving guidance, it must be heard.

Many will believe what we say, many will not
Many have long awaited for the Word that we brought
I am the Messiah, sent here to save mankind
Those who follow my Father's Words, will not be left behind.

I will be with you for only a short while
When I am gone, you will continue to walk many a mile
To spread my Father's Word, which you have embraced
For our love in you has been gently placed.

There will be many trials and tribulations awaiting for us
But unto my Father, we will place our trust
For he is my Father, the Lord Almighty who reigns in heaven
And I am the Lord Jesus Christ, only through me all sins will be forgiven!

Don't Cry Any Tears For me

Don't cry any tears for me
Just because I cannot talk
Soon I will be in heavens gardens
And peacefully, I will walk.

Don't cry any tears for me
Just because I am not awake
Though it may seem, I am sleeping
I can see the angels smiling, waiting for my soul to take.

Don't cry any tears for me
Just because my time with you was only for a short while
The angels say heavens children are waiting
As they gently fly around me making me smile.

Linda Laybolt
Whispers From Heaven

Don't cry any tears for me
For I will not suffer anymore
Only peace and love, I will find
As I enter through heavens doors.

Don't cry any tears for me
For I want you to be happy not sad
Think of me with a smile upon your face
And the happy memories, we once had.

Don't cry any tears for me
This is not our final good-byes
In heaven, I will be waiting for you to arrive
Then, we can cry and have tears in our eyes.

Don't cry any tears for me
Safe in the loving arms of Jesus, I will be
Home is calling, I must go
The beauty of heaven now awaits for me.

Safe In The Arms Of Jesus

The sun is brightly shining
As I slowly step outside
But my heart cries for comfort
From deep within on the inside.

There are times, I feel so all alone
Those are the never-ending days
That I really need to feel your presence
And your boundless loving ways.

Refuge is mine there always to behold
When the heart cries from deep within
For into your loving arms
You will always gently tuck me in.

Comfort for the soul
Compassion to the unsettled mind
All this love unfolds
Within your arms, I find.

Tears will subside
Taking away all the hurt and pain
Surrounded by your divine love
Contentment is mine, once again.

My worries and fears are yours
As my burdens, you willingly release
As you hold me next to you
Once again, I will be at peace.

With endless love
You are there, when called upon
Reaching out with loving arms
You are the one, I always depend on.

Having faith and trust in you, My Lord Jesus
You come to my rescue
Your unconditional love never ceases
And that's why Jesus, forever I will love you!

Take Time To Smell The Roses

Reflections of days gone by, echo through my mind
Days come and go but memories linger, never being left behind.
As time continues to elapse, contentment fills the soul
Life has had its toll, the body now feels somewhat, complete and whole.

The never-ending days of youth seem to have flown by
Like the colours of a rainbow, that disappeared in the sky
Just like the years, many seasons have passed by one by one
Without taking notice, where they ended or even begun.

Linda Laybolt
Whispers From Heaven

The seasons were created with so much beauty, it sometimes makes a person wonder
With so much to be seen in each, why are they so short and not longer
The Lord took much care and thought of each season
That is why each is made with such splendor, for a reason.

The long cold winter season has come to an end
The awaited spring has slowly arrived and is about to begin
The little bird prepares to build a nest, hidden high up in the tree
As I take time to look around, so much is happening for me to see.

Spring is a natural rebirth of plants and animals alike
Renewal of nature as it first started, just as a bird takes its first flight.
Where empty branches once stood on trees, buds have now start to dwell
Shortly turning into leaves, the Lord has so many stories to tell.

The warm sun and rains of summer emerge, as spring starts to disappear
Birds sing their lullabies, flowers surface from below the ground, appearing everywhere.
The cooler winds of winter and summer have departed like their seasons have too
Replaced by a soft gentle breeze, with endless skies of white puffy clouds and colors of blue.

There is so much of summer to see and so much to do
When the Lord created it, he was thinking of me and you
For it seems, that summer is the season, he thought so carefully of
In a lot of ways, it reminds me a little bit of his heaven above.

But as the saying goes, all good must come to an end
Summer eventually descends, while fall will ascend
But just like summer, it's worthwhile taking the time and having a second look
Beauty is here to be seen like looking at breath-taking photos in a book.

Linda Laybolt
Whispers From Heaven

A time to give thanks for all the harvests of summer, a time for good-byes
The birds will migrate south, taking flight in the skies
The cooler days have caused the leaves to slowly disappear
While the rest of nature prepares for winter, this season will abruptly appear.

But winter too, by the eyes of the beholder, can be seen as a wondrous sight
The moon and stars are amazing to see, on a cold winters night
It's a time to reflect on the seasons that have passed by you
And all the changes that the seasons and you have passed through.

The Lords Seasons have embedded many memories in your heart
That was his intentions, of his mighty works from the very start
When you look back, the seasons have not passed by you
For you stopped as many others do, to take time to smell the roses too!

The Lord's Club

There is a club that can be found in many a town
I've known for years, that it has been around
The admission to join it is absolutely free
Many say, it's the in place to be!

All over the world, the club can be found
All are welcome to come have a look around
Some say the membership is in the millions
But I think it's the high millions or even the billions!

It does not matter if you are rich or poor
All are welcome to come through the door
Even if your feel, you are too sad and blue
Come anyway, our leader will take care of you!

Linda Laybolt
Whispers From Heaven

Our leader is absolutely divine
He is well known for being loving and kind
He will take anyone under his wing
That's why we call him Our Mighty King!

He is always there to listen with an open ear
He is full of compassion but you must be sincere
He's always ready to give help whenever he can
He's been the leader, since the club began!

You will find that our leader is so full of love for all
He'll even pick you up if you happen to fall
And if you feel you can no longer walk the road you've come to
With his loving arms, he will gently carry you!

There is no love on this earth, that can compare
Than that of our leader, yet even today many are so unaware
He is the shining light for all to see
He'll take your burdens and set your spirit free!

I hope that you consider at least to check it out
And find out for yourself what the club's all about
This is the only club on earth, full of so much love
Named after our leader, that's why we call it "The Lord's Club!"

The Lord Looked Down From Heaven

The Lord looked down at earth from the heavens above
Some of his animals that he created out of love
Had disappeared and become extinct from this place
Sadness appeared all over his face.

He thought well, let me have a look at my mighty forests
Some he could not find, for they no longer exist
Where trees once stood, now was empty land full of space
Again, sadness appeared all over his face.

Linda Laybolt
Whispers From Heaven

It looks awful hot down there, he thought
Global warming has put most of the people in distraught
Look at all those strange chemicals filling the sky, it's a disgrace
Again, sadness appeared all over his face.

Look at those rockets shoot up high in the sky
And when they reached their destination, he could hear his children cry
I guess my words of love fell upon deaf ears and was not embraced
Again, sadness appeared all over his face.

My beautiful world, he sighed, where has it gone?
With all that noise, it's hard to even hear the little birds lovesong.
Even some of my people and animals cannot find a clean watering place
Again, sadness fell all over his face.

I would look at the Tribes of Israel, but them I cannot see
Many generations have passed but they can't hide from me
I know there have been many changes but them, I don't even see a trace
Again, sadness appeared all over his face.

And then it occurred to the Lord, I know my people are here
They come to me in prayer, for their voices echo throughout the air
Just then the Lord heard a little voice praising him with so much grace
It wiped away all sadness from his face.

I guess I was just looking in all the wrong places for my children
They are everywhere here but the places I've been
There was so much love being sent in prayer for him to embrace
That now, all you could see was a glowing smile upon the Lords face!

Thy Will Be Done

With my all my heart
I give my love
To you, my Most Loving Lord
Who reigns in the heaven's above.

Father of mankind
Creator of all things
With a heart of gold
So much love he brings.

You are the Almighty Lord
You are my One and Only
Idols cannot give comfort and love
When I feel sick and lonely.

Blessed is your Holy Name
For I would never use it in vain
Keeping the Sabbath Day Holy
Is not that difficult,to ascertain.

Loving and Honouring my Parents
True unconditional love is your way
Do Not Kill, for you my Lord
Is one thing, I always will obey.

Your Commandments Lord, are clear and precise
They are so easy for all to understand
Do Not Committ Adultery
Is one big reason, we wear a wedding band.

Do Not Steal, for it is wrong
To take something that does not belong to you
Do Not Lie, one little lie leads to another
These words are so ever true.

And last of your Commandments is Do Not Covet
My thoughts and desires will never be to hurt any one
All of your Commandments show me your love
That's why I will always obey your Words,"Thy Will Be Done".

The Vine And The Branches

The Lord Jesus looked around at all his disciples
He had something very important he had to say
You could see the sincerity in his words as he spoke
Obey the words " Love One Another As I Have Loved You," each and everyday.

He compared himself to a bush and said
I am the true vine and I bear fruit for all to see
Any of my branches that bear no fruit, my Father cuts off and throws away
The ones that bear fruit, he prunes so more fruit will grow on the tree.

My Father is the gardener and one thing he has taught me
Is that one of my branches alone, will not bear anything
No fruit will grow without the vine
This is why, what my Father has spoken to me, I've told you everything.

If you keep your faith and teach others my ways
And my words of love which I have taught you all
You can ask my Father for anything in my name,you wish
He will give to you, even if your request is big or small.

This is my Father's glory, that you bear much fruit
Showing yourselves to be my disciples, in all you do
As my Father has loved me
So have I loved you.

Linda Laybolt
Whispers From Heaven

I will call not call you my servants no more
A master does not tell his business to them
Everything that I have learned from my Father
I have made known to you, it all came from him.

There is no greater love that a friend can give
Than to lay down his life for his friends whom he loves
Keep my love in your hearts always
Just as I have in my Father, in heaven above.

I am the vine and you are my branches
I remain in my Father means we love each other
I love all of you and all of you love me
That is why I want you to obey my Words always, "LOVE ONE ANOTHER."

Are You Ready For The Lord's Return?

Who knows, maybe this will be the year
Prophecy has it, that the time is near
Many will be surprised and so unready
When the Lord returns in all his glory, Are you ready?

No one knows when the time will be
There will be no place to hide or flee
Many will try to get away
From the Lord Jesus on that glorious day!

Many will shout with joy, the Lord has come
Others because of their evil ways will become fearsome
There won't be a place of solitude for you
Only for those whose hearts are pure and true!

The Lord many times has said, Seek and ye shall find
He is the only one who can give you full peace of mind
Is it really worth taking the chance, hoping that he will not show
The Lord will return in full fury to gather his flock, you know!

Linda Laybolt
Whispers From Heaven

One day you will look up and there he will be
With his army of angels filling the sky for all to see
Trumpets will blow and the angels will shout out
The Lord Jesus is here for all to hear, in the world throughout!

There will be no need in crying to the nations to protect you
For the King of Kings will be seen all over the world in full view
There will be NO nailing him to a cross, just like they did before
The ultimate price for our sins, he's already paid for!

Now is the time, to seek the Lord's word
Don't listen to others because they don't believe what they have heard
The Lord is forgiving and full of so much love for you
All can enter his mighty flock, but your love for him must be honest and true!

So then, it's up to you if you want forgiveness of your sins
To have the Lord in your heart and always carry his love deep within
Wouldn't it be nice to have peace of mind and be waiting for that glorious day
That the Lord Jesus returns, who knows my friend, it could be today!

Snowflakes And Angels

Outside my window, snowflakes gently float by
The north wind roars, the trees sway, up high
Slowly reaching their destination on the ground
Beauty and elegance, earthward bound!

Sometimes, when I look at the snow as it falls
I think of God's Angels, dressed in white by all
Armies of Angels descending from Heaven, I see
To watch over us, sent by Our Lord, The Almighty!

Linda Laybolt
Whispers From Heaven

No one knows exactly how many in numbers, they are
But then again, no one has ever been able to count all the stars
Only the Lords knows the exact number of them
His Loving Angels, watching over us, sent here by Him!

Everywhere on earth, they can be found
Sitting or walking beside us, not making a sound
Angels of comfort, Angels of love
Angels of the Lord, sent from Heaven above!

Angels have long been around long before man
That was the Lord's plan, before the world began
God's messengers and servants, full of love and devotion
Continually praising Him, with deep emotion!

The beauty of an Angels lies deep within ones mind
How does one describe a spirit which God made so Loving and kind
Beautiful Angels with big white wings
Forever, singing praise to Our Lord, King of Kings!

Angels in Heaven, Angels on Earth
Nothing could ever measure up, to your loves worth
You watch over us by day,you watch over us at night
Forever, you'll remain in God's shining light!

Snowflakes from the skies, to the earth given
Or is it Angels sent to the earth, from God in Heaven
Whatever it be, you both come from above
And you both come to us, from Our Lord Of Love!
r without His great love for you
You would have no memories, to think of!

Your Loving Guardian Angel

Walk with me, even if its just for a short while
It definitely will be worthwhile and perhaps I will make you smile.
I have so much to talk to you about
So many stories, you should check me out!

I have white shiny wings and a face that constantly glows
So don't be afraid of me, for you my love flows
Although you cannot see me, I am always with you
Whether sad or happy, or cheerful or blue.

Think of me this way, I am somewhat like a parent
The only difference is, I am mostly transparent
When you were born, I was there
Carefully watching over you, with tender, loving care!

When you were a baby, I sat by your bed
While you slept, my loving wings around you, were spread
I watched you as you learned how to walk
I laughed as I tried to figure out your sweet baby talk!

I never left your side when you were feeling ill
And to this day, I am around you still
There is nothing of your childhood, that I won't remember
To me, you have become my precious family member.

Through all the good times, I was there with you
In sad times, my love and comfort saw you through
Now, you are all grown up standing in front of me
But you are never alone, beside you, I will always be!

In so many ways, you have become my dear child
When I first saw you, my heart smiled
We have been through a lot together, you and me
A long road still awaits us, yet to be!

Linda Laybolt
Whispers From Heaven

Whatever path in life you choose to take
I will be there when you sleep and when you awake
The Lord sent me to watch over you, whatever you decide to do
I am your guardian angel and I truly love you!

Mark 12:13
And you shall love the Lord your God with all your heart and with all your soul and with all your mind and with all your strength.

Three Little Children Who Found Love

I'll never forget the first time, I laid eyes on her
As she rocked, she sang about her dear mother
Three years old, long blond hair with big blue eyes
My heart is a crying for you Mama, so sad were her cries!

Her older brother and sister played quietly on the floor
But their little sister, you could not ignore
She sang cries from her heart, for here Mama that day
The sweet little girl, who had come here to stay!

I was told the three of them would be staying a long while
As I looked at the three of them, not one had a smile
The looks on their faces, wandering what was to be
Three lost, scared little children was all I could see!

How do you explain to a child, you'll never see your Mama again
When all you can see is the heartbreak and pain
That day three little children came into my care
Three little children full of sadness and despair!

The days turned slowly into weeks, how fast time flies
The children wake up with smiles at sunrise
But little Sabrina still rocks with tears in her eyes
My heart is a crying for you Mama, so sad are her cries!

One day a worker came with good news to share
There's a couple coming to meet the children so prepare
If they decide to adopt them, they'll be leaving here one day
And taking them with them, forever to stay!

For months, the couple came to visit, brightening the childrens days
They had grown to love these people, I can honestly say
When the day came for them to depart
I was so happy they found a home, but sadness filled in my heart!

Its been years now but they write me from time to time
The mother once wrote, I'm so happy Sabrina is mine
She no longer rocks and sings,with tears in her eyes
She says she's found her Mama, and she longer cries!

TWO SECRET MESSAGES

LOVE is a big word, I've heard
OTHERS is the Lord's Word.
VIRTUALLY the Lord means everyday
EVERYDAY is the Lord's way.
TESTIFY in the Lord's love
HONOR the Lord in heaven above.
EMBRACE the Lord,never to depart
LOVE the Lord with all of your heart.
OBEY the Lord is to adhere
RIGHTEOUS the Lord will always stay near.
DEMANDS the Lord's request to you
WHOLE-HEARTEDLY the Lord wants your heart to be true.
ILLUMINATE the Lord's light will not disappear
TRUE the Lord loves the sincere.
HUMILITY the Lord requests this
Always the Lord brings to you bliss.
LOVED the Lord loved his disciples
LORD the Lord set forth his values and principles.
OBSERVES the Lord laws is The Ten Commandments
FAITHFULNESS the Lord commands.
YOU the Lord loves always
ONLY the Lord will never sway.
UPHOLD the Lord's upholds the righteous who have fear
RIGHTEOUSNESS the Lord keeps the righteousness near.

Linda Laybolt
Whispers From Heaven

HEAVEN the Lord reigns in this Holy Place
EMBRACES the Lord's grace.
ALWAYS the Lord says he expects
REVERENT the Lord seeks respect.
TRUST the Lord wants trust with all of your heart
SPREAD the Lord's word is love and will never depart.
ONLY the Lord Jesus can wash away your sins
UTMOST the Lord wants to give you love, deep within.
LOVE the Lord with all your heart, soul, and mind
ASKING the Lord will give his love, he will not leave you behind.
NEVER the Lord says forget him, whatever you do
DEMANDING the Lord will not bring his love to you.
MESSAGE there are two more in this for you to see
IS hidden , so look carefully.
NOW if you find them, please write them below for all to see
DONE is this poem in which the Lord inspired me!

God Lives

The sun is starting to set as I walk along the long dirt road
Each step I take is slower carrying the heavy load.
Sometimes, I wonder why life can be so hard to endure
Why can't a person live a life of just being safe and secure.
A life without all the worries for you and me
A world to live in, as calm as could be.
A world of peace, with wars unheard of
Where everyone gets along, it's called brotherly love.
No more sickness or pain from within
A world where everyone is free of sin.
Unfortunately, we once had a place like this
But sin stepped in and it no longer exists.
Sin took away the way people act, think and feel
Leaving mankind with so many horrors yet to reveal.
Sadly, many have forgotten about God, leaving Him behind
To them, He does not exist; "The Creator of Mankind."
Yes, it's a long road that each of us must walk each day
But God is always beside you, never far away.
The load may be heavy with many burdens to bare
But God is more than willing to take them, just whisper a prayer.
No matter where you are, God always will hear you

Linda Laybolt
Whispers From Heaven

God Loves you and wants you to "Him" to turn to.
May Gods Love shine upon you, each and every day
And many Blessings from Him come your way!

Rain, Rain Go Away

The stillness of the air
Means the rain is lurking near
Thunder roars off in a distant
But I don't know exactly where!
The chimes are softly ringing
A black bird nearby sits quietly, looking around
Sounds that floated earlier through the air,
Are now nowhere, to be found!
Even the skies that were once blue
Are now dark, grim and grey
The calm before the storm
A sure sign that rain is on its way!
Sitting and awaiting, on my porch
All nestled in my rocking chair
All nature that surrounds me, also awaits
Just by the quietness in the air!
Even the flowers appear to be looking at the sky
All standing upright, straight and tall
It's almost as if they have inside perception
That soon God is going to let the rain fall!
Once the rain begins, so does the storm
It may strong with rage, fury and high winds
Or it may be mild and weak with passion
We just need to wait it out, till it ends!
When all has calmed down, the storm is over
All of nature becomes renewed again
Sunny skies lay ahead in the days to follow
All plants and animals flourish, all due to the rain!
So the next time, it looks like rain
Don't complain because you wanted a sunny day
Be grateful for all the tiny drops of water, that God has sent
And never say the words, Rain, Rain Go Away!

Linda Laybolt
Whispers From Heaven

Harmony, Peace and Love

Harmony is when we all agree
Peace is no hostilities, stress or anxiety
Love is an emotion of devotion or strong affection
The three entwined is a strong connection!

Live a life in harmony with all and you will find
Peace in your heart for all mankind
Love one another each and everyday
Harmony, peace and love is the Lord's way!

Linda Laybolt
Whispers From Heaven

Our Lord and Creator,

We are sending you this prayer today
There are a few things that we would like to say
We want to talk about harmony, peace and love
That our world does not want to take hold of!
We hear your people as they talk about these things
And the sadness to their hearts, without it brings
Some of your people have turned deaf ears to your Word
For a lot of mankind has not listened, to what they have heard!
If we live in harmony, then we live in peace
And if we live in peace, all hatred the world would release
If there is no hatred, then there is only love
This is the world you created for us, not one to dream of!
Why is so hard for some to understand
That harmony, peace and love is your Law of the Land
Why can't people get along with each other
When your command is to Love One Another!
We wish you would come and straighten this mess out
Your world needs harmony, peace and love, without any doubt!
There is one more thing we want to say to you
And that is Lord, we all love you!

And The Little Birds Sang Their Sweet Lullaby

They have been here since the beginning of time
Maybe they were created to fly with the angels, we so greatly adore
Most sit high in the trees chirping and singing their sweet lullabies
Although they may seem small, sometimes their sweet voices are hard to ignore.

When the Lord created the earth and the heaven's above
Much thought he put into everything full of his love
And when it was all said and done, the angels could be heard singing close by
And up high in the trees, the little birds sang to him their sweet lullaby.

Linda Laybolt
Whispers From Heaven

Many animal sounds the Lord did hear
He created them all with a different sound to the ear
But the one that stood out the most, seem to come from the sky
For up high in the trees the little birds sang to him their sweet lullaby.

Little voices echoing throughout the air for him to hear and embrace
Pleased the Lord so much that a smile appeared on his face.
For with every single day that passed by
High up in the trees, the little birds sang to him their sweet lullaby.

Then one day, the Lord did not hear the little birds sing
And a feeling of emptiness to his heart,it did bring
So he went to the little birds and said Why ,Oh Why
Do you not sing high in the trees your sweet lullaby?

The little birds looked at the Lord for they thought they had did something so very wrong
We have not sung to you our lullaby song
Because lately, we noticed a tear in your eyes
And we are sorry for making you sad with our sweet lullabies.

The Lord started to laugh at the little birds so
They are tears of happiness and of joy, for you make my heart glow
Would you please sing for me, he said with a sigh
For I really do miss hearing your sweet lullaby.

And so the little birds started to sing to the Lord every day, you see
That is just the way, that things were meant to be
So now, when you hear a little birds voice echo throughout the sky
You'll know that high up in the trees, the little birds are singing to the Lord their sweet lullaby!

The Homeless Person

You pass me on the street all the time
In the pouring rain and in the hot sunshine
You never would consider saying hi or hello
Coming and going in a big rush, to and fro.

I know that you constantly avoid where I am at
You would never stop and have a chat
I may not be as well dressed as you in clothes
Mine are raggedy and dirty,full of holes.

If I said to you, let's go for a cup of tea
I know you would look strangely at me
You would not want me, to be seen by your side
That is a fact, that can't be denied.

There are times in winter, I stand here in the freezing cold
Wishing I had something hot to drink in my hand to hold
Instead I stand here being completely ignored
Ever so lonely and ever so bored.

You say get a job and get off the street
Do you think I like living out here on the concrete?
I can't help it if misfortune has come my way
Perhaps tomorrow, will bring a better day.

There is nothing better. I would like than a warm place for me to live in
Anything would be better than sleeping in a garbage bin
It's too bad I couldn't put my shoes on you
Then, you would see the hardships, that I go through.

I am a real person with real feelings, you know
Begging for food and money,hurts my heart so
So the next time you see me, please don't just rush by
Even if you don't stop, can you please say hi.

The Heart Of Mary

Dragging an old wooden cross through the crowd
The laughing and mocking was extremely loud!
She watched holding back the tears in her eyes
She did not want her Son to see her cry!

Her heart was crying; inside she screamed in prayer
The Mother of Jesus; in complete despair!
Even though she had known this day would come to be
She begged to God, to set her Son free!

Jesus was just a man of barely 33 years old
All through time, His story has been told!
All our religious holidays revolve around Him
The Son of God who was born in Bethlehem!

Tempted by Satan, with many hardships to face
Traveling mostly on foot; from place to place!
It was not an easy life; for Him to endure
The message remained the same; whether rich or poor!

Yet, Jesus continued His journey to teach
Many crowds gathered to hear Him preach!
Healing the sick, performing miracles along the way
Speaking The Word from His Father in Heaven, far away!

Now nailed to a cross, with two thieves on Calvary Hill
Obeying His Father; a plan Jesus had to fulfill!
A crown of thorns upon His head; suffering in great pain
As sad as it is, The Son of God did not once complain!

As Mary watched her Beloved Son Jesus die that day
She knew that this was meant to be; it was the Lord's Way!
When He was laid to rest in the tomb that mournful night
She did not know a miracle was soon to be, within her sight!

Jesus died on the cross that day; so all sins would be forgiven

Three days later, Jesus came back to life before ascending into Heaven!
2013 years ago, Mary's heart was broken on what we call Good Friday
But Joy was in her heart; three days later on what we call Easter Sunday!

Prophecy had now been fulfilled!

John3:16
For God so loved the world that he gave his only begotten Son, that whosoever believes in him should not perish, but have everlasting life.

The Kingdom Of Heaven

As the fresh smell of the morning mist fills the air
Gods presence can be felt everywhere!
The dawn is on the horizon, a new day is on its way
Good Morning Lord, What can I do for you today?

Your thoughts always reflect unto the Lord
You want to make this day right, and live by His Accord!
Even when you are busy or just relaxing at ease today
You take the time to talk to Him and pray!

Just when you least expect it, something happens to you
An angel appears before you, completely out of the blue!
A set of stairs appears out of nowhere, within your sight
It looks dark but far off is a brilliant, glowing light!

You proceed to walk the steps, the Light engulfs you
Beyond all thoughts, it is something you must get to!
At the end of the stairs, you walk right into the Light
And there it is....Heaven is within reach and your sight!

Linda Laybolt
Whispers From Heaven

The huge pearly gates are wide open for you
The Lord Jesus, Your Lord & Saviour is in full view!
He has His arms held wide open, you feel humble and mild
Softly he says, "Welcome Home My Child!"

You are overwhelmed, the excitement is too much to bare
You feel high on a cloud, like you are walking on air!
This is the place you longed for and always wanted to be
All your burdens are gone forever, your soul has been set free!

High in the trees, little birds gaze up to the sky
Perched on branches, singing their lullaby!
All throught the air, angels voices can be heard
Carefully you listen as they sing, word by word!

Even the flowers and the trees seem to dance
Everything has to come to life at first glance!
The Glory of Heaven is beyond anything in your sight
Since you walked out of the darkness, into the light!

You soon forget this morning getting out of bed
Wondering to yourself, what your day will be like that lays ahead!
Little did you know that today on earth was your last day
That by tonight, you would be Home in Heaven to stay!

No more tears, pain or sorrow, here you will find
Only tranquility, harmony and peace of mind!
A warm feeling embraces you, something undreamed of
After all, This is The Kingdom Of Heaven & God Is LOVE!

The Shepherd

I am the Shepherd; you are my flock
Beside you, I always will walk.
I will never desert you; but you may stray
Stay with me; I will show you the way.
With me; you shall not want

Linda Laybolt
Whispers From Heaven

Stay with the world; the devil will taunt.
When you are troubled with worries or fear
Don't get fooled by anyone; I am always near.
When you feel no strength; to move along
I will carry you; till the feeling is gone.
When you are weak or ill; I will tend to you
Whatever happens; I will see you through.
I will never forsake or leave you; I love you
You are part of my flock; I am here to come to.
You may think that I am not watching; but I see all
Nothing can be hidden from me; big or small.
Abraham's Seed is my family; you are mine
Remember my teachings in the Branches and the Vine.
The world has changed drastically over the years
What looks real to you; may not be what it appears.
You have to search for answers; go back to the start
Open your eyes; listen to your heart.
I am the Shepherd, Lord Jesus; you are my flock
Beside you, I always will walk!

GOD IS LOVE

1 John 4:8
Anyone who does not love does not know God, because God is love.

Just sitting here thinking about the Love
Jesus had for His Father in Heaven
To come here to earth so willingly
And suffer as he did; so all sins would be forgiven!

Persecuted by man; tempted by Satan
Yet, Jesus continued His journey to teach
Traveling mostly on foot; from place to place
Many crowds gathered to hear Him preach!

Linda Laybolt
Whispers From Heaven

Ridiculed by many; yet He had many followers
It was not an easy life; for Him to endure
Spreading His Father's Word; throughout the land
The message remained the same; whether rich or poor!

Although His life here on earth was short
He never once betrayed; His Loving Father in any way
Even in His darkest hours; as He suffered on the cross
His Divine Love for His Father did not fade away!

We all speak of Gods Love; the Divine greatness it is
But do we really comprehend or truly understand?
Jesus knew what truly awaited back Home for Him
Coming from Heaven; He knew firsthand!

Loving My Father was the Word that Jesus conveyed
Love One Another, Jesus taught; as I have Loved you
The Divine Love that awaits; for you in Heaven
Only The Lord Jesus, The Son Of God truly knew!

1 John 4:7-11
God Is Love

7 Beloved, let us love one another, for love is from God, and whoever loves has been born of God and knows God.
8 Anyone who does not love does not know God, because God is love.
9 In this the love of God was made manifest among us, that God sent his only Son into the world, so that we might live through him.
10 In this is love, not that we have loved God but that he loved us and sent his Son to be the propitiation for our sins.
11 Beloved, if God so loved us, we also ought to love one another.

And God Spoke: Let There Be Light!

I've watched sun rise in the early morn
Remaining exquisite as the first day it was born
Each day it rises, a new day begins

Linda Laybolt
Whispers From Heaven

While somewhere else, another day ends!
People often talk, what is this life is all about
As they go about their way, day in and out!
What about your day? Will you shine in the Light?
Or will you remain in the dark, out of sight?
Blessed are those who walk in the Light of the Lord
Blessed are those who live by His accord!
Let Gods Love surround you, each and every day
May the Light be brighter today than that of yesterday!
May you feel the Lords presence where ever you may be
May you walk before Him, Humbly with Pride and Dignity!
May you carry "The Lords Love" always in your heart....
May your Faith, Hope and Trust in Him, Never Depart!
Let The Lords Light shine upon you, even in the darkest hour
He holds All Wisdom of this world, along with the Greatest power!
Remember each day as the first light appears in the sky
That the Lord in Heaven is watching over you, from way up high!

Are You Ready?

Are you ready to leave this earth?
It's been your destiny, since your birth!
Will you feel happy inside, when the time is near?
Or will you have regrets, perhaps fear?
When the time comes, to meet Your Lord
Can you say to Him, I've lived by Your Word?
Can you say I've done lots for my fellowman?
I did my best, according to God's Masterplan!
Will you be able to look at the Lord in the face
Without feeling you failed Him or feel out of place?
Will you tell Him that you are so thankful to Him
For all the pain, He suffered for Your Sins?
Will you say, Thank You Lord for sticking with me
For shining Your Light, so I could see!
Will you Thank Him for the times, He carried you?
For all the Compassion, He bestowed upon you!
But Most Importantly, Will you declare your Love?
To Your Lord Jesus, In Heaven Above!

I Know, I Am Safe, Next To Him!

In the midst of the raging storm,
I feel deep comfort, from within
Darkness may fall, surrounding me
But I know, I am safe Next To Him!

The Lord is My Shepherd
I shall not want, with Him!
I am part of His flock
I know, I am safe, Next To Him!

The Lord is My Strength and My Salvation
He is My True Friend, I Trust only Him!
Whatever road, my life follows
I know, I am safe Next To Him!

The Lord is My Shield and Protector
Refuge is mine to Behold beside Him!
My Protector stands beside me all the way
I know, I am safe Next To Him!

The Lord is My Provider and Helper
All Blessings come from Only Him!
There is nothing I need that He cannot Provide
I know, I am safe Next To Him!

The Lord is My Everything
Mighty and Powerful describe Only Him!
He is My Healer of All things
I know, I am safe Next To Him!

The Lord is Everlasting to Everlasting LOVE
He is Kind, Compassionate and Forgiving
He is Holy, Righteous, and Real
I know, I am safe Next To Him!

Linda Laybolt
Whispers From Heaven

The Lord, My God is My Saviour
I would be lost, Without Him!
I will Love My Lord Always and Give Praise
I know, I am safe Next To Him!

The Lord, My God Is Perfect and Real
Nothing would exist, Without Him!
Alpha and Omega, The Beginning and The End
Who would not feel safe, Next to Him!

Rays From Heaven!

Surrounded by fields and trees
The little country church sits
High on the steeple is a cross
Rays of light on it transmits!

Fields of hay and straw are on one side
An old worn-down barn is on the other
Once attended by many on Sundays
Horse wagons unloaded here, one after another!

A rope attached, to an old rubber tire
Can be found out front in a big old tree
Once it was the playground for children
After the service, while the parents drank tea!

Now the little old church sits empty
Between the fields, all on its own
Its doors have been closed for a very long time
But the Rays from Heaven, means its never alone!

The grass around it may be worn and brown
It looks abandoned by the naked eye
But somehow, I think the angels are in it "Rejoicing!"
From the the Divine Light that shines from the sky!

PRAISE THE LORD, YOUR GOD!

Praise the Lord, Your God!
Praise Him, today and everyday!
Praise the Lord, Your God!
Never turn your back...and walk away!

The world is His
so are WE
Everything that ever WAS...IS
And yet TO BE!
Lord of Lords,
King of Kings,
FOREVER
He shall reign!

Chained by Sin, My Lord Jesus Loved me
No more worries,
Of Eternal Death!
I will sing Praise
Forever unto Thee!
On the cross,
My Lord Jesus saved me!

In a cruel world,
Without conscience or shame,
My Lord Jesus,
Freely came!
With a love for all in heart
For all of Mankind
He paid for all SINS
Not even I was left behind!

Praise to you, Most Holy Lord
Let me live my life by your accord!

Linda Laybolt
Whispers From Heaven

Let me have compassion,
For those all around me.
Let me walk with a clear conscience
No wrong doings,
I want you to find!
Let my LOVE radiate,
For Your Word,
Is to love ALL!

Belief is something
Promised to me
That Heavens Gates
Will be open for me!
If I humbly pray
And truly believe
The Lords Blessings,
I will receive!
Armored with Love
To all in His sight
Freely Giving,
Everlasting Light!
To everyone who earnestly seeks Him
The Lord Shines down upon them!

Let my faith, for you come shining through
For there is only room, for one God
And THAT IS YOU!
Let me obey, Your Commandments everyday
As Moses did,
Showing us Your Righteous Ways!
Full of Mercy and Passion,
My Lord Jesus IS
For saving me,
My heart is filled with Bliss!
Sing! Sing! Oh Give Praise!
To Our Lord, all of your days!
Praise! Praise! Oh Give Praise!
All through Hid Kingdoms
He spreads His Divine Love!

Linda Laybolt
Whispers From Heaven

Out of Love,
He freely paid, the debt
For Me and You!

Let me manifest, my Love for you
In all that I say and do!
Let me give hope, to those with fears
And let me help wipe, away the tears!
Let me Honor You, with respect and Dignity
For All Eternity!
But most of all, Lord
Let me carry your love in my heart!
My Lord Jesus,
Your Love and Faithfulness
Are forever with me
Let me forever follow You!
With You leading the Way
Forever Prasing You!
Forever Loving You!
Lift up your voice unto the Lord!
FOREVER, PRAISE HIM!
Now and Always!

A Vision Of Hope

It's another very cold winter night
The winds are whipping up and howling
Dropping the temperatures to 30-35 below zero
The wind is going right through me
Chilling me right to the bone.
As I shiver from the cold
With all my clothes on, it does help at all.
I try to find some corner or nook
To get out of the howling winds.
As I sit, my mind is slowly going numb
I start to dream of holding out my hands

Linda Laybolt
Whispers From Heaven

Begging for money from people that pass by me.
I dream of a warm place with a warm blanket
For me just to stay the night.
I open my eyes just for a moment
I see my guardian angel standing before me
Telling me, that it is alright!
It is slowly getting near dawn
For I hear people moving and going about their way.
As I struggle to get up, to go on for another day
I must hold out my hand again
In hopes, that I get some money
In order to get a cup of coffee somewhere.
My mind is still numb from the long cold night.
Somehow, I am not sure whether I am dreaming
Or still awake.
Struggling to take each step as I try to push forward
Hoping that God will call me Home soon.
then, I would always be warm and have no pain
With no more hunger even
As I look up into the sky and Heaven above
I slowly pray for The Lord to come and get me....
And take me Home, To His Father's House!

John

Jesus, The Messiah

I came into this world knowing my fate
For many years, patiently many did await!
Phophecy foretold of the Messiah that was to come
And when I did, it was believed by only some!
I did my best when I was here
Many a hardships, I had to endear!
I devoted most of my life to my Father's Word
Teaching about His Love, to those who had not heard!
I healed the sick, whether rich or poor
Yet, with all the miracles, many wanted more!

Linda Laybolt
Whispers From Heaven

I choose twelve Disciples, I knew one day I would be gone
I taught them all I knew, so they would carry the Word on!
I wept when I heard about Lazarus being dead
I prayed to My Father then Lazarus, Come Out, I said!
I walked on water to save my Disciples, My Dear Friends
On a cross, I died for my Friends, in the end!
Satan tempted me many times, throughout my earthly days
Not even he could stop me, from teaching my Father's Loving ways!
Jesus of Nazareth, the Messiah of the Mankind, I am He
I died on the cross many years ago, yet I live for Eternity!
I came to earth and lived a short while amongst you
I brought with me Eternal Life, for you to come to!
Just as Lazarus, no one that believes in me will ever die
A new life awaits you in Heaven, death is not the final good-bye!
Alpha and Omega, I am the beginning and the end
The decision is yours, it's all up to you, My Friend!

The Shooting Star

I saw a shiny light fall down from the bright lit sky
As I was watching many shooting stars go by
This one was way different than all the rest
For my eyes could not believe, what was about to manifest!

I heard a gentle voice say, I am here, have no fear
You are not alone, I have always been near
I heard your cries float throughout the air
Then I heard you call my name, while you shed your tears!

In humble prayer to me, your heart cried out
You finally came to me, without any doubt
So I am here to let you know, I'll be your guiding light
Just give it a little time, things will be alright!

I could feel the warmth of His love, as it surrounded me
The chains of anguish were lifted, I was now free
Safe within His arms, comfort and compassion were all mine
The love that illuminated deep within my soul, was truly divine!

Ever since that night, I know I am never alone
For any child of His is never left on their own
With me he will always be, so grateful that he rescued me
My Lord Jesus, my love is forever yours, for all eternity!

Love In Your Heart

How does a person get love in their heart, she cried out
I want to know the truth, what people are talking about!
Love is an emotion which left me, many years ago
Can I get it back, I am so lonely, I need to know!

He looked at her with compassion, he could see the tears in her eyes
She had not come to him in a long time, but he could hear her cries!
As he placed his loving arms around her, he spoke in a soft tone
My child, he said, what makes you think you have a heart of stone?

I have watched you over the years, you were never alone
I have always been here, watching the many seeds of love, you have sown!
Who was the one that looked after her mother, staying by her side?
For years you let life slip by, taking it all in stride!

Who was the one that gave up her dream to go to school?
Because family was more important, it was your golden rule!
Who was the one that stayed up night after night rocking a sick child
And patiently sat at home, while her husband ran wild!

Who was the one that volunteered at the senior home?
Also the hospital, and the girl scouts, just to mention some!
Who is the one that can see beauty in just about everything?
And gives comfort to all that need it, taking them under her wing!

My Child, you do not have a heart without love in you
You are at a place of time in your life, you need me to turn to!
I have waited so long now, for you to come to my door and knock
But you did not have knock, it is always open anytime, for you to talk!

Linda Laybolt
Whispers From Heaven

It does not matter, whether it be day or night
I am always here waiting full of love, with my guiding light!
With the warmth of His Love completely surrounding her, she knew she wrong
And she replied, My Lord you are right, I have love and been loved, all along!

Little Flower

Little flower, little flower, arise and awake
The sun is shining and its past daybreak!
Open your pedals wide for all to see
For you never know, who is looking, down at thee!
Little flower, little flower, take a look around you
Surrounding you, fields of beauty, in full view!
So many smiling faces looking at each other
Field after field, one after another!
Little flower, little flower, your colors are so amazing
When I look at you, my eyes will not stop gazing!
I can tell that you are as happy, as can be
When I look at you, you are smiling back at me!
Little flower, little flower, I'd love to take you home
But I think I will leave you here, and let you, grow some!
But I will be back for you soon, this I know
And home to my Garden in Heaven, with me you'll go!

The Voice

I heard a soft voice whispering my name,
I looked around to see where from it came!
But no one was in my sight that I could see
Was this voice really calling out to me?

So I kept on walking till I reached the place
Where peace and quiet, I could fully embrace!
The waves rolled in, the waves rolled out
Then I heard my name again, without any doubt!

Linda Laybolt
Whispers From Heaven

This time it was definitely my name that I heard
So I sat quiet to see if I could hear any words
Sounds of laughter was coming from the sea
Was it the waves, really laughing at me?

Then I heard a voice call out my name again
I knew from the tone of it, it understood my pain!
I heard Him say to the waves, be gone all of you
And with those words, the laughter withdrew!

I sat there helpless, not knowing what to do
Then he stood in front of me, in full view!
I tried to get your attention earlier, he said
But you did not stop, you went full stream ahead!

Why is it, when I speak, you do not listen to me
But you listened to the waves, calling you from the sea!
I speak to you all the time, my voice is here
But you do not pay attention, do you not hear?

I looked up, I could see the sadness in His face
I felt so ashamed, my heart was full of disgrace!
Lord I am so sorry for not listening to you
Can you forgive me and let me start anew?

Then He placed His Loving arms around me
My Child he said, I have already forgiven thee!
From now on, listen to the voice from deep within
For it is mine talking to you, he said with a grin!

Hold Onto My Hand

Hold on, wait for me, don't leave me standing here
Don't go away, stay with me, don't disappear!
Hold onto my hand, my heart is full of love for you
Hold on, my Child, you need someone to turn to!

Linda Laybolt
Whispers From Heaven

You say you're lost and all alone, no one cares about you
Well I am here to tell you that, none of this is true!
Reach out for me, so much comfort I can give
Compassion is waiting here for you, yourself you need to forgive!

So hold onto my hand, I'm reaching out but you must too
With me, a new beginning of life awaits to start anew!
A life surrounded by love, peace and contentment can be yours
I can see for you, openings of many new doors!

You feel hurt, confused and all torn up inside
You've given up on life, you feel you have been tossed aside!
You just want it to end, there's no place left to run and hide
I can set you free from all the tears, you have cried!

I want you to know, with you I have always been
You have never been alone, I've been here since your life begin!
You are part of me, when you hurt, I hurt too
So let me lead the way, let me the one that you turn to!

So reach out your hand, mine is waiting for you
There will be no regrets, I'll see you through!
I'll shine my guiding light, for you to find your way
Beside you I will walk, with you I will always stay!

So hold out your hand, let me come into your heart
I know once you do, we will never part!
I have so much love waiting for you, so much to share
My hand is reaching out for you, because I care!

A Father's love is always there and will never fade
Don't turn your back on me or be afraid!
You are my Child, always have been and always will be
My love awaits for you now and for all eternity!

Lord, You Are Holy!

Searching always for answers
Where has all the faith gone?
I am your past, present and future
Forever, I will live on!
Revelation 1:8
I am Alpha, I am Omega
Who is, who was and who is to come, the Almighty
Revelation 22:13
I am Alpha and Omega
The first and the last, the beginning and the end

I had a dream, about you Lord
I had a dream, about you being adored!
All in Heaven, worshipped and gave glory to you
As you walked around, in my full view!
A feeling of Love engulfed my soul
For the first time in my life, I felt whole!
My eyes filled with tears, the closer you got to me
Your face for the very first time, I was about to see!
I felt so ashamed, for all the wrong things I had done
I wanted to hide, but there was no place to run!
I hung my head in guilt and wept out loud
Unto my knees I fell, amongst the crowd!
I had always believed that you were my Saviour, My Lord
I had always tried to live, by your accord!
But, I was not worthy enough to be here, at all
This place was for followers, like Simon and Paul!
Then, I heard a soft voice say, Stand up, My Child
When I did, you looked at me and smiled!
There you stood before me, face to face
Holding out your arms, for me to embrace!
I was at peace, I whispered Lord , Thank You
For saving me and all the pain, you had to go through!
Smiling at me, he replied, This is your future home, Heaven
When you come here, you know all sins are forgiven!
Then, I woke up from my sleep, to my surprise
I realized that this dream had come to an end, to my demise!

I got down on my knees and started to sing
Lord, You Are Holy! Lord, You Are Holy!
My Dear Saviour Jesus, so much happiness you bring
Lord, You Are Holy! Lord, You Are Holy!

My Friend, My Lord Jesus Died For Me

Long ago, My friend passed away, on a long dark day
Right up till the end, He suffered in a horrible way
He never complained about all the pain, He was going through
He knew all along, it was something, He had to do!

Some thought it was a big joke,as he lay there dying
While others stood by in shock and crying
Here was a young man at the age of thirty-three
Waiting for the Lord, to set his spirit free!

There was no pain medication given on that day
Not a thing at all to stop the hurt and make it go away
The blood was slowly flowing from his body, everywhere
Sometimes, death can drag on, full of despair, so unfair!

He prayed to His God, in Heaven above
He prayed to His Father, whom he dearly loved
The perfect man innocent of all sin, so it is said
Now hung waiting for death, a crown of thorns placed upon his head!

Hail! King of The Jews was written in bold letters, for all to see
Placed above His head, how they laughed at He
How mean they all were to my friend, how sad the words they threw
In all his suffering, he prayed to His Father, Forgive them for what they do!

Yes, my friend, My Lord Jesus suffered in pain
Upon a cross on Calvary Hill, he was slain
He came to us with love for all in his heart
He died for us all out of a love that will never depart!

Linda Laybolt
Whispers From Heaven

Never again will My Lord Jesus wear a crown of thorns
In heaven he reigns forever, loved and adorned
Hail! King of Kings, of all heavens and earth, we proclaim
Blessed Be, Thy Holy Name!

My Lord Jesus gave me eternal life, when he died
Never again, will he be mocked and cast aside
My Lord Jesus, My Saviour and friend, forever to be
Died on the cross that day but now lives forever, for all eternity!

A Child Found His Way Home

A man walked in your house today, without making a sound
Being very quiet, just to have a look around
No one noticed when he walked through the door
No one noticed, he had never been here before!

As he sat down, he could see only one thing
A statue of a man saying King Of Kings
Just who was this man he thought to himself
He was not dressed like a man of wealth!

The pastor was just starting his sermon and began to speak
Heaven is a place for the humble and meek
And then he proceeded to tell the life story of Jesus, Our Lord
As if it was the first time to all that had not heard.

He talked about Jesus teaching about love
He talked about His great love for His Father in Heaven above
He told about how he came to earth from heaven
So that all sins would be forgiven!

He spoke about his teachings to all that he gave
He spoke about his love for his people, he had come to save
He told of all his healings to the sick and the poor
He spoke sadly that it was not enough, they wanted more!

Linda Laybolt
Whispers From Heaven

He told about how they had turned their backs on him
How he was nailed to a cross, after all he done for them
He had tears in his eyes that flowed down his cheek
Making it difficult for him to speak!

He said, Jesus paid the ultimate price for our sins
Yet, today, there are people that will not let him within
By within, I mean in their hearts to believe
The love he holds for all that is free to receive!

Jesus, Our Mighty King sent from heaven above
Sent by Heavenly Father to share His Words of love
How sad it is to think of the world's loss
Our Beloved Saviour, the Son Of God nailed to a cross!

The man who had entered the church shamefully hung his head
Tears rolled down his face, from what the preacher had said
Now I know why Lord I was lead to this Holy place
I've been missing something from my life, that is your grace!

I have been wondering around lost all these years
Full of anguish, hatred and tears
But today is the last day on this earth, I will ever roam
Today, My Dear Lord, I have finally found my home!

Jesus, My Lord

Blessed be Thy Holy Name
Forever King, Thy Kingdoms to reign
My Precious Lord Jesus
Thank you for coming to us!

Down from Heaven, you came
With Heavenly Father's word, to proclaim
In the darkness of the night
You shined your guiding light!

Linda Laybolt
Whispers From Heaven

You taught us about love
As it is in Heaven above
Reaching out, touching hearts
Spreading a love, that would never depart!

Compassion was your way
Each and every day
You healed the sick and weak
Taught us to be humble and meak!

Teaching us about faith and trust
To do what is right and just
You conveyed Heavenly Father's Word
To all that had not heard!

Obeying your Father to the fullest
Humbly and earnest
The love you carried within
Completely innocent of all sin!

The Saviour of all Mankind, My Lord
Ignored by some, by others adored
Willingly gave His life for us
My Precious Lord Jesus!

Echoes Of Love

Every prayer and their words, the Lord embraces
Ascending to Him, from so many places
Voices throughout the air, Echoes of Love
From everywhere, to Our Lord in Heaven above!

Echoes of song and praise,
About Gods Loving ways
Echoes of happiness, joy, and delight
That all here, is alright!

Linda Laybolt
Whispers From Heaven

Echoes of sorrow
For a better tomorrow
Echoes of grief
From those who seek relief!

Echoes of fear
That the Lord is closeby and near
Echoes of despair
That they can no longer bare!

Echoes for those sick and in pain
That the Lord will bring comfort, once again
Echoes for friends and loved ones
Soaring to Heaven, one by one!

Echoes of heart break
From the quiet and meak
Echoes of loneliness
To fill the void and emptiness!

Echoes of hopes and dreams to share
All wrapped up in a little prayer
Echoes of the faithful
From the heart and soul!

The Lord loves to hear from us in prayer
Our Father in Heaven, really does care
When you say a prayer, listen for the echoes of love
Being sent back to you, from Our Lord in Heaven above!

In Heaven, The Angels Sing

Praise! Praise! To Our Lord, Our God
Lift up your voices, strong and loud
Praise! Praise! To Our Mighty KIng
In Heaven, the Choirs of Angels sing!

Linda Laybolt
Whispers From Heaven

Love Our Lord, in Heaven above
Love Our Lord, who gives us love
Love! Love! Our Lord with all your might
Who keeps watch on you, day and night!

Rejoice your spirit, in song and praise
Rejoice to Our Lord, all through your days
Rejoice! Rejoice! To The Lord Almighty
Who reigns forever and will always be!

Proclaim that Our Lord is the one Most High
Proclaim to all, Our Lord's return is nigh
Proclaim! Proclaim! The Lord gave his life for us
Proclaim it all, for Our Lord Jesus!

The angels sing praise in Heaven above
Forever, singing Praise of His Great Love
Praise! Praise! To Our Lord Jesus, Our Mighty King
In Heaven, His angels will always sing!

Someday, I Will Be Home To Stay

This life is a long and weary road
And the burdens can be a heavy load!
With so many huge mountains to climb
Forever, facing me, time after time!
Many tears over time, I have cried
No matter, how hard I have tried!
So much shame, has followed me along the way
And still does, to this very day!
So much hurt, refusing to leave me
Someday, I will be set free!
So much pain, in everything I do
Sometimes, I feel so blue!
But then, you came along
And made me strong!

Helping me cope, day to day
Showing me a better way!
Loving you with all my heart
From you, I'll never part!
And when my life is over and done
I will come Home, to my Loved One!
No more tears, no more shame
No more hurt, no more pain
No more long and endless days
For I will be Home to stay!
Heaven, the angels and I will sing
Halleluijah! To Our glorious King!
Heaven, I can't wait to come to Thee
My Dear Lord, is waiting there for me!

No Falling Rain From The Sky, Only My Tears

I said to myself, Why did this have to be?
Mankind's sins were finally set free!
A crack of thunder soared across the sky, with His final breath
Finally, no more suffering as He departed into death!
Three hours before His death, darkness revealed itself, in full view
The earth roared as it shook the mountains, stones split in two.
The veil in the temple was torn in two from top to bottom
Yes my anger was unleashed, but nothing like Sodom!
My God, My God, Why hast thou forsaken me? My Son cried!
No answer, only silence from here, on the Heaven Side!
My Dear Son, Jesus, whom I love and adore
Your cries from your heart, I could never ignore!
The last days of your life, I suffered along with you
My heart was broken, for all you had to go through!
I know you gave your life willingly for mankind, without any fears
That is why,on that day, "There was no falling rain from the sky, Only my tears!"

My Special Little Friend

I had a friend when I was young
She was about the same age as myself
She would meet me out back of my house everyday
I can barely remember exactly what she looked like
Except for the glow she had all around her!
Everyone claimed that she was imaginary friend
That I had made her up in my mind
But now that I think about it, especially the glow
Was she imaginary at all?
She had beautiful colors all around her body
Now, I hear nowadays that was her aura
But then they say everyone has an aura
So where did this little friend of mine come from?
I grew up in a small village, where everyone knew everyone
And no one had ever heard of, or seen this little girl!
Except for me, my special friend Cathy!

Little girl, little girl! Where did you come from my friend?
Everyday, I meet you out in my yard never failing without end!
Your eyes light up and you have a radiant smile
When we see one another, even if it's only for awhile!
Little girl, little girl! I can't wait to see you everyday
I look out the window and watch for you to come to play!
We play so many kinds of different games all the time
High up in the trees, sometimes we climb!
Little girl, little girl! We laugh, joke and tell stories galore
We share many secrets and so much more!
When you run, your long blond hair also glows
As the rest of your body, from head to toes!
Little girl, little girl! My very special friend
All will know you are real, not my imagination, in the end!
Gone but not forgotten are those happy times, from long ago
For you remain in my heart my sweet friend Cathy, forever so!

The Beauty And Grace Of Fall

The long days of summer have quickly, passed us by
The heat from the sun, no longer radiates from the sky
The warm, gentle, soothing breeze that filled the air
Has been replaced with by a cool wind, for us to endear!

Gracefully, another season has quickly come and gone
Along with the little birds, that filled the trees with their song
A time for harvesting the fruits of summer, winter is on its way
But for the time being, fall is here for awhile to stay!

Most say that fall is a season, where all the beauty of nature
Comes to an end, but I see it as the season of most grandeur!
The vibrant, brillant tones of different colors of the leaves
Proudly display beauty that God has created, for us to perceive!

The green grass and flowers that flourished, in the fields yesterday
Still shine in radiance, although the colors have faded away!
The small brook where you could sit and enjoy, natures at its best
Is now peaceful and quiet, but still exquisite, even at rest!

The animals of the wild, prepare for the long winter ahead
Most spend their days gathering food, while others prepare to hibernate instead
The salmon make their last journey of life, from the sea to spawn
To the many rivers ancestors travelled, to ensure their species live on!

High up in the mountains, the peaks cover with snow
The trees on its side sway with the north wind, as it blows
But down in the valley, people prepare for the harvest
The fruits of the vine are ready, which God hath so generously blessed!

The barns are filled with hay and straw, the animals have been brought in
Although it is fall, one never knows when snow will begin.

Linda Laybolt
Whispers From Heaven

Soon it will be Thanksgiving Day, a day of feast with a turkey all dressed
A day of gratefulness to the Lord, being thankful is deeply expressed!

Fall is such a magnificent season, with so much beauty to embrace
Created by God for us to behold, a treasure of greatness full of his grace
Enjoy the fall season to the fullest, there is so much to see out there
Wherever you look, God's love shines in fall everywhere!

*John Donne once wrote, No spring or summer beauty hath seen such grace,
As I have seen in one autumnal face!

Gone, But Not Forgotten

Soldier! Soldier! Who fought bravely for my country land
With dignity, pride and reverence, forever you will stand!
Departed from life, but forgotten, you will not be
I know not your name, but you are remembered by me!

Soldier! Soldier! It was so many years ago
You left your home, foreign lands to go!
Willingly, you left your loved ones behind
Devoted solely to your God and Country, deepest in mind!

Soldier! Soldier! You were so young, as many were
Little did you know, what was to take place or occur!
Old and new friends became your new family,one after another
Closely knit and known as, your trusting Band of Brothers!

Soldier! Soldier! The cost of my freedom was so high
It saddens me that you had to be amongst, the battle cry!
The dark days and long nights, that you had to endure firsthand
Is something a Soldier of War, could only possibly understand!

Linda Laybolt
Whispers From Heaven

Soldier! Soldier! So very few of you, returned home
Broken and wounded, burdened with unwanted memories for some!
Home to freedom and family, a prayer answered to few mothers
But the battle cry continued for life, from your departed Band of Brothers!

Soldier! Soldier! Forever Valiant! Forever Brave!
The gift of freedom, to the future, you dutifully gave!
In Flanders Field row on row, Bands of Brothers now lay
Forever remembered, amidst the poppies, on this Remembrance Day!

Soldier! Soldier! Your war is over, but a new one continually surfaces, so it seems
A world Full of Peace and Harmony, nowadays is still not the impossible dream!
Everyday brave new soldiers fight for the Freedom of Others, holding the Vision of World Peace in their mind
Carrying your Legacy of Love for God, Love for their Country and Love for all Mankind!

Another Day

In the early morning hour
As I sit and plan my day
Wondering what to do first
What I must get done today!

As the sun slowly creeps light, up the horizon
Darkness fades, night finally comes to an end
I wonder what this day will bring
Perhaps, a visit from a long lost friend!

As I toil away in the warm sun
That the morning has bestowed upon me
My thoughts remain, about today
Just how hot it is going to be!

Pushing through my work
Trying to get everything done, that I must do
But as the day drags on, I soon realize
There are some things, that I won't get to!

As the day comes to an end, I sit and reflect
Upon the the things accomplished today
I silently pray in the back of my mind
Thanking God for all the blessings, sent my way!

I also give thanks for being able to work
For the strength, He has given me on this day
The day has quickly gone by, the sun starts to fade
Another night of darkness is gradually on its way!

Looking around at the beauty and magnificent colors
I gaze upon the flowers and roses, that surround me
They seem to stand out, above everything else
Stunning and exquisite, elegant and free!

Thinking how God has created, all this beauty
Brings tears to my eyes, when I think of thee
Thinking how Great the Master's plan was
Especially when He created you and me!

By John

As I Wander

As I wander
Through the fields
Filled with grass
Weeds and flowers
As I smell
The fragrances
Of the grass

Linda Laybolt
Whispers From Heaven

And the flowers
And see the beauty
Of all around me
In a dazzling display
Of colors around me
In blues, whites, yellows, reds
Pinks, lavenders, and purple
As I wander
I come upon a brook
Listening to the water
Running by over the rocks
Watching some small fish swim by
Listening to the frogs
Among the cattails
Upon the opposite shore
Noticing birds of different kinds
Flying around and about
As they chirp and sing
Being busy, feeding their young
As they pick and gather food
As I wander along
I come upon the forest
With so many kinds of trees
Some small and straight
Some so big and majestic
That makes me feel
So very small among them
As I sit and rest
Under the shade
Of a big oak tree
It makes one wonder
How God created
Everything
From His Great Master Plan
To create such beauty
And also to feed all
The animals and birds and insects
So that all would have
Lots and lots to eat

Linda Laybolt
Whispers From Heaven

As I wander slowly back
Night is beginning to fall
As the sun slowly dims
Over the horizon
In a majestic display of colors
In reds, pinks, yellows and oranges
I lay down in the field
Looking up at the sky
The moon is coming up
Now it is dark out
The sky is filled
With a dazzling display of stars
With some bigger ones among
The thousands of small ones
Moving about the Milky Way
And the Big Dipper
And so forth
Making me wonder
How majestic God's plan has been
To create the sun by day
The moon and stars by night
For all of us to see
Knowing deep within my heart
That only God
Could have created all this
For He created us!
The animals, the fish, the birds
So always remember and know
That Our Lord God
Is Master of All
So pray to the Lord
For He cares for all
Big and small!

By John

Morning Prayer

When I arose this morning
I prayed to the Lord, My God
Good Morning Lord!
What can I do for you today?
For all things you do for me
Day after day after day.
Lord you have been with me
Since the day, I was born.
Lord you have walked with me
Every step of the way.
when I wandered off the path
You Lord guided me back.
When I was in grief and pain
Lord, you carried me, through it all.
For Lord, without your help and guidance
Out of love for me
I would not have made it at all.
Your love for me
Is so abounding in every way.
Lord, you are so forgiving
For forgiving every time we stray
Away from Thee.
You have taught me
To live with the good
And bad things in my life.
Enduring hardships in this life.
To make my belief
Grow stronger and stronger In Thee My Lord, My God.
you have given me
The ability to serve Thee in my way
Longing to serve Thee
Better and better in every way.
As I prayed to Thee, My God
waiting to see
as the day unfolds
what I can do for Thee.

Linda Laybolt
Whispers From Heaven

My Lord, My Saviour, My God
Praises in the highest
For Thee only, My God!

By John

My Lord In Heaven

Lord, as I go about my day today
There's so much to you, I want to say!
With so many mysteries, waiting to unfold
For so much to us about you, yet has not been told!
Answers to the questions I have, seem to becomer clearer
As I age in years, as the end of life draws nearer!
My soul is full of contentment, as each day passes by
Your presence is felt deep within, always near and closeby!
The days seem to go by more swiftly now, than before
Each moment of time is precious, I long for more!
Everything that happens seems to be taken, like a grain of salt
No more pointing fingers, as to who is at fault!
Love is in my heart at full blossom, like the flowers are
Green meadows stretch beyond imagination, wide and far!
Beauty of your wondrous works, stand out more to the eye
Admiring every little thing, as my day passes by!
Trials and tribulations, still follow me day to day
They are no problem now, with you leading the way!
I am so grateful for all that you have given me
Through my eyes, I wish the whole world could see!
As I write my poems, which are all inspired by you
I pray your endless love in the words, shines through!
All praise and glory be given to you!
My Lord in Heaven, How I Love You!

Good Friday, The Day Of Love

Very shortly, it will be Good Friday once again
Christians around the world will remember the cross of pain
It is the day Our Lord Jesus was crucified
The day Our Lord Jesus paid for our sins, when he died!

It is the saddest day for me to think about
The Son Of God suffering in pain for me, without any doubt
I have often wondered why it is called Good Friday
The day mankind turned their back on Jesus, in such a big way!

But then, I got to thinking about it and came to the conclusion
Dying on the cross was Our Lord's decision
Many times he had escaped being arrested and caught
But this time was different, this time he did not!

He had spoke many times of this day that was to come
Even in days of old, it was written by some
The Prophet Isaiah wrote about Jesus, the Messiah of earth
Many, many years long before his blessed birth!

Jesus prepared His Disciples during His final days
Speaking of many things for them to remember, now and always
Never once did he complain about how difficult His life had been
He spoke of His Heavenly Father's Love, right up till the very end!

Jesus came to earth, sent by His Father in Heaven above
Willingly he gave His life for us, willingly he gave out of Love
A love for mankind, a love for His Father
An unconditional love, beyond any other!

So when we really think about it, it should be called Good Friday
It was a day of sadness, a day of love, it was the Lord's Way
For without that day, we would still be living in sorrow
With no hopes of eternal life and a brighter tomorrow!

Isaiah 53: 1-20

WELCOME HOME, MY DEAR CHILD

As I take the few last steps, of this mighty stairway
I can see a huge set of gates, swung open in front for me
It looks so beautiful, beyond those pearly gates
My heart is jumping, with joy and glee!

As I get closer to the gates, I see a man standing there
He is watching me, as I take each step, in stride
He looks to be about six feet tall, with long dark hair
His body glows, just as the bright light beyond the gate inside!

As I take a glance ahead of me, I see only a couple steps left
I am so nervous now, I would love to be able to hide
But as I look into the eyes of that warm, Loving face
I see it is My Dear Saviour, with arms open wide!

Tears fall down my face, as He takes me in His arms
All I feel now is Love, from His warm embrace
All those mixed feelings, have now disappeared
Peace and contentment have taken their place!

He says that He has been waiting for me to climb the stairway
His voice is dominant, yet gentle and mild
As He lets go of me, He quickly grasps hold of my hand
With a warm Loving smile, He softly says
"Welcome Home, My Dear Child!"

A Heart Full Of Love

While walking through my garden of what was once filled with radiant flowers
I notice a heart full of love has come my way
For on this chilly late fall day,there on a leafless bush
Stands alone,an elegant red rose in full bloom for me today.

Shocked and amazed, my eyes must be playing tricks on me
I kneel down beside it, gazing at it for awhile
As I gently touch its delicate stem, I feel all warm and happy inside
For a heart full of love fills my face with an over-whelming grateful smile.

Then I say to myself, pick it or just let it be
Different answers ponder around in my mind
I can't leave it out in the cold to dwindle away
For a heart full of love, I must not leave behind.

As I place it carefully in my very best vase
Thoughts run through my mind, how a red rose means love
Thank you Lord for this beautiful flower that forever,I will cherish
For this heart full of love,could only be sent, by you in heaven above.

If Only

If only, I could reach out
And touch your heart
Your world would be like day, full of light
Not as night, gloomy and dark.

If only, I could reach out
And take away all of your sorrows
Tears would be a thing of the past
Only brighter tomorrows.

Linda Laybolt
Whispers From Heaven

If only, I could reach out
And take away all your pain
There would be no more suffering
Only skies of blue, without any falling rain.

If only, I could reach out
And take away all hunger of this day
Never again,would we hear a child cry
Only smiles and laughter,should it be any other way?

If only, I could reach out
And stop all these needless wars
It would put an end to all anguish and fear
I really don't think,that's a whole lot to wish for.

If only, I could reach out
And fill the worlds heart with God's love
Peace and harmony,would rule the earth
But until that time, it is something for me, to think about and dream so of.

Smile

Smile! Be kind, I know you have it in you
Let that hidden love shine through
Don't be crabby and grouchy today
Stop letting Satan have his way!

Smile as a new day is about to start
Let others know, you still have a heart
Being mean is not very nice
C'mon now, take some good advice!

Stop letting every little thing bother you
Worrying will only make you sad and blue
Get out of the house for awhile
Just like you, someone out there needs a smile!

And if you can't go out, don't feel left out
You are never alone, beyond all doubt
Just ask the Lord to be with you today
Then "SMILE" as He sends His Love, your way!

Remember Yesterday.....

Remember yesterday,
When we were once young, full of play
The world was ours, not a care to worry about
We'd run and jump till we were all played out!

Getting up and going to school
Not missing a day was the Golden Rule
Walking the long road there in rain and snow
No matter what, we had to go!

Recess and lunchtime, we all got to play
Outside of course, was there any other way?
When the school bell rang for us to go in
We knew school books waited for us within.

There was no computers back then
Just paper, crayons. pencils with no pen
We paid fully attention to what our teacher said
Or across our desk came the yardstick instead!

Sure now and again, we'd play pranks on the teacher
Only to find out, she was a real mean creature.
Standing all day in the corner was not fun
Or getting the strap, one by one!

But then again, things always weren't all that bad
We all learned to write on that writing pad!
We learned everything we needed to know
In that one room school house, many years ago!

Linda Laybolt
Whispers From Heaven

Now when I look back, I am grateful for all we had
It may not have been much but I am Glad
We learned to respect each other and get along
Which wasn't so bad, am I wrong?

The Lords Prayer was said everyday
Not cast away like today!
The Lord was part of our school
Why did they change the rule and be so cruel?

Reflections Of the Days Gone By

Thinking about the days, of no return
The days when we were young, so much to learn
Sadly those days have slipped by us, so fast
Leaving us with only, reflections of the past!

The older we get, it seems the more luggage we pack
If only we could open up the past, thus return back
To our days of youth, of innocence and carefree
Would we change the past, or just let things be!

All of us, at one point would like to go back again
To the tranquil blue skies, but not to the falling rain
The joyous and cherished times, remain an open door
Trials and tribulations are tucked away, in a closed drawer!

Some of us have a past, that we would like to forget
Full of shame, sorrow, and actions, that we regret
Wishing that we could go back and make amends
To all we have hurt, strangers, family and friends!

While for others the past remains, a life full of bliss
Days are spent endlessly, full of reminisce
No regrets or sorrows, a past full of love
No thoughts whatsoever, "I wish I would of!"

Linda Laybolt
Whispers From Heaven

Yesterday the paths that laid before us, looked so long,
At times the decision was tough, which one to travel along
Now we realize that time, never stands still
Dreams are now are visions of the past, left unfulfilled!

What seemed to look like alot of years, awaiting in time ahead
Now are decades that have passed, being very short instead!
Where has the time gone, you often ask yourself in thought of mind
Somehow it drifted by you, with it dreams and visions lingered behind!

Nowadays, all you have is relections of the past to dwell upon
Memories of what once was, embraced in your heart tag along
Forever yours to hold in your heart, never to fade or disappear
Reflections of your past, always remaining close and near!

Christmas Poems:

MISSING:

Feeling a little overwhelmed, now that Christmas is near
Or are you feeling a little lonely, this time of the year
Come celebrate Christmas with me, the sign proudly displayed
Everyone is welcome, Do not be afraid!

The holiday season starts earlier every year
Months before December, the stores are in high gear
Pictures of Santa and decorated trees, appear everywhere
People are rushing around before the big day draws near.

Linda Laybolt
Whispers From Heaven

Lights are lit up all over the place for all to see
Putting most people in the holiday spirit, agree?
All you hear is holiday music, that's the way it goes
Even the television is overloaded with holiday shows.

Whatever happened to the old days of Christmas gone by?
I don't see any pictures these days of a bright light in the sky!
Nor do I see angels lit up or the Nativity scene laid out!
Has everyone forgotten what Christmas is really all about?

And did you hear the new saying is not Merry Christmas but Happy Holidays!
Why are they taking the Christ out of Christmas away?
Maybe people have forgotten about me and why this holiday exists!
I am Real, Loving and Kind; not by any means a myth!

Years ago I was born in Bethlehem, a gift to Mankind of God's Love
I Am Jesus, Gods Beloved Son, sent from Heaven Above
I am what Christmas is all about and there is no other reason
So come celebrate Christmas with me at my home, this season.

FOR MORE INFORMATION CONTACT:
JESUS, LORD OF LORDS AT ANY OF MY HOMES

Mary's Gift To Jesus

I've been waiting for your arrival, ever since Gabriel appeared to me
I constantly dream about you in my dreams every night
My love for you is endlessly growing, as a mother's love should be
I long to gently touch your little face as I hold you in my loving arms ever so tight.

Although I did not know it, angels stood by closely that day
Into Bethlehem as Joseph and I made our way
At the Inn, not a room or bed could we find
For you my unborn baby, who was sent from heaven to save all mankind.

Linda Laybolt
Whispers From Heaven

Weary and tired, I told Joseph, I can feel the angels nearby
My spirit filled with comfort and love, surely this must be the night
Suddenly, I saw a bright star appear, lighting up the whole sky
I knew then, it was Your Heavenly Father, letting me know everything was alright.

All heaven's eyes watched as the angels gathered round me in prayer
For the safe arrival of you, my sweet little one
In a crowed stable, while the world stood so unaware
You were finally born, The Messiah, God's Heavenly Son.

Off in a distance, I could hear the trumpets and music as it filled the air
Heavenly hosts and angels were rejoicing with praise and song
A little baby called Jesus was now in my tender, loving care
Once seated beside God in heaven, now earth you do belong.

I often wonder why God chose me to be your earthly mother
By God's grace, you were sent to me from heaven above
Throughout the years, as told many times by the prophet's, one after another
You are the Saviour of the world sent by divine love.

But for now, Baby Jesus, you are my sweet little one
All I have is bands of cloth to wrap you and a manger for you to lay in
I know it's not much for the King of Kings, God's only son
But all I have to offer you is the love, from my heart deep within.

It's going to be a long journey that you enter upon
There are those that will not believe that you are true
Only Our Heavenly Father knows what path you will walk on
But for now, you will stay with your mother, for I dearly do love you.

Linda Laybolt
Whispers From Heaven

Christmas Without Baby Jesus

Just imagine how lost and sad
All of us and the world would be
If Baby Jesus had not been born
Many years ago, for you and me!

Christmas would not definitely exist
Something completely, unheard of
We would still be separated from Our Father
With no hopes ever seeing Heaven Above!

We would still be watching and praying
For a Saviour to come and deliver us from sin
But with all the years that have passed by
The world may have forgotten about Him!

But Baby Jesus was born in Bethlehem
All Praise and Glory Be Given Unto Him!
Our Heavenly Father sent us a gift of Love
Who opened the gateway to Heaven Above!

This Christmas celebrate the Birth of Baby Jesus
The Saviour of the World, who came to earth for us!
The little baby that was sent from Heaven Above
To fill our hearts, with Everlasting, Divine Love!

Three Wise Men

The angels proclaim the Messiah is on earth
Baby Jesus is here, for Mary has give birth
Love and peace, you are going to now find
For he is here to save all mankind.

They told us to follow a bright shining star to get to him
In a manager is where he lays, in Bethlehem
We gathered up our gold, myrrh and frankincense

Whispers From Heaven

And off to Bethlehem we went.

We found him exactly where they said
In a manager made out of straw is where he laid
We could feel the cold, even though we were inside
Quietly he slept as we knelt down by his side.

Mary and Joseph watched carefully as he slept
We knew that with them, Baby Jesus would be safely kept
Here lay this tiny little baby sent from heaven
To take away the sins of the world so that all would be forgiven.

As we were kneeling down beside him, he opened his little eyes
Here knelt three humble men now, who at one time thought they were very wise
When he smiled at us, our eyes wept with tears at the chosen one
Here lay before us, The Messiah, God's one and only son.

We gave unto him, our gifts that we did bring
And when we did, we could hear the angels sing
Glory be to all in the heavens and here on earth
For this is the night of Our Dear Saviour's birth.

Baby Jesus, The Newborn King

Look high up to the sky tonight
See if you see a star shinning OH SO BRIGHT!
For this is the night that A KING WAS BORN
So many years ago, that the world has come to adorn!

A little baby that came from Heaven to us
That changed the world forever, Baby Jesus!
The red carpet was not rolled out for Him
Actually, there was no inn for Him to be born in Bethlehem.

His parents Mary and Joseph could only find a stall
No cozy room or bed, for Him at all!
Just a barn full of animals, not fit for a King

Whispers From Heaven

But they made do, with no complaints about anything.

He was wrapped in sworns of cloth very carefully
And placed in a manager of hay so gracefully.
Not one cry from the Little King as He looked around
All the animals watched, without making a sound!

Here lay The Son Of God in the poorest of places
Yet the stall was full of peace and love on all faces.
No, it was not a great place for any baby to be
But high up in Heaven, all was singing with glee!

Tonight the Messiah has been born, the angels sing
Hallelujah To Our Majesty, Our Newborn King
And God smiled from Heaven with Love in His heart at His Little Son
For God had sent Him Full of Love, Baby Jesus, "The Chosen One!"

Grandchildren Are Forever

Sweet is your smile, as that little voice of yours
Young and innocent, learning new things
Always happy to see me, no matter what
Grandchildren are earth's little angels, without wings!
Getting into mischief, so it seems, all the time
Climbing on tables and countertops, with no fear
Flushing toys that fit down the toilet
When no one is watching and the coast is clear!
Pulling hair and slapping one another
Fighting over a doll, book or toy
Yet, to sit down and read you a book
You are as quiet as can be and such a joy!
To see you dance and twirl across the room
Brings a huge smile to my face
The sweet memories, you give to me

Linda Laybolt
Whispers From Heaven

Are mine forever, to embrace!
Combing your long hair and braiding it
Trying to make you sit still as you move about
Telling you how nice it looks
Because soon, I know, you will take it all out!
Watching you laugh and play in the tub
Splashing the water, all over the floor
Never wanting to get the shampoo, rinsed out of your hair
Bath time for you is fun, but for me a wet chore!
But all in all, you are still little angels to me
Those loving little smiles melt my heart away
Along with the many hugs and kisses, so full of love
Is just what Nannie needs, to brighten her day!

My Twin Girls

My sweet darling daughters, how much I love you so
Right from the first time I laid eyes on both of you, which does not seem that long ago.
Beautiful tiny little beings sent from heaven above, just to me
My two little blue eyed babies with blond hair, Jessica Lynn and Jamie Leigh.

The years when you were small seemed to fly by so fast
I often wish I could go back when you were small into your childhood past.
It seemed like one minute you were in diapers,crawling around the floor
Then, the next thing I knew you were on your way to school heading out the door.

I used to laugh at you both walking on your toes like ballerinas instead of your feet
Then, there was the excitement of getting dressed to go trick or treat

Linda Laybolt
Whispers From Heaven

The Easter Bunny was another big day
But the most popular of all was Christmas, so you would happily say.

Jamie was the little lady and always wore a dress
While Jessica wore baggy pants and shirts, there was no one she wanted to impress!
Because you are identical, not many could tell you apart
Sometimes, even I had trouble but my guess turned out good on the most part!

Then, there was those awful teenage years
I thought that there would never be an end to all my tears
But that was just a stage of life you both had to go through
To drive me up the wall and keep me feeling blue!

Now, you are both grown up and say you out on your own
You both have your own little ones, but you still have not left the nest, cause you're always on the phone!
But it does not matter, I am always happy to talk to you, too
Because I am your mother and no matter what, I will always love both of you!

Never Let Go Of A Dream

I have thought about you as long as I can remember
You became a part of my life that I cannot explain
I knew back then,I would search to find you
And when you were nowhere to be seen, my heart filled with pain.

Once upon a time long ago,I dreamed of a special love
One who held the missing pieces to make me complete
Childhood dreams,imaginative and pure
Embedded deep within my heart,ever so discreet.

Rainbows and fairy tales, knights on white horses
Young and innocent, dreaming what was to be
But time sneaked in, the years slowly slipped by
Dreams filled with clouds, becoming impossible to see.

Linda Laybolt
Whispers From Heaven

I have watched the pages of my life turn one by one
Many filled with laughter, along with the tears
Memories from a lifetime, so many stories to tell
So many changes took place over the years.

I thought to myself, now it's all said and done
Until a new door opened and a dream once forgotten from so long ago
Suddenly re-appeared from beneath the clouds
Gnawing at me, begging please don't let go.

I knew who you were as soon as we met
The one I had once searched for, dreams really do come true
For you held all the missing pieces that make me complete
And that my darling is one reason, why I so deeply love you.

Dreams never cease, they sometimes get tossed aside
They may take a lifetime to come into full view
So never forget a cherished desire
For when it finally comes along, you'll know like me what exactly to do.

Dedicated to John

Leaders of the Nations of the World

Leaders of the Nations of the World
Let peace reign upon the lands
Let the world stop fighting
For something, noone understands!

Leaders of the Nations of the World
Not one person on earth wants war
Only you can change the way we live
Is that too much for people to ask for?

Linda Laybolt
Whispers From Heaven

Leaders of the Nations of the World
Do you enjoy watching children die each day?
Yet you proclaim, they are our future
While every day, thousands disappear and fade away.

Leaders of the Nations of the World
Why must each of you want to rule one another?
Why must you have the best of nuclear bombs?
When in reality, everyone just wants to get along with each other.

Leaders of the Nations of the World
Why can't you just help one another out?
When one Nation needs help, only a few come to the rescue
While the rest of you are scheming to hurt others, beyond any doubt.

Leaders of the Nations of the World
No parent wants to see their son or daughter die
Only you can stop the needless slaughtering
Only you can stop a mothers cry!

Leaders of the Nations of the World
We live in the year 2015, the so-called modern age
Yet around the world, it looks like we are going back in time
With all the chaos caused by your deplorable rage!

Leaders of the Nations of the World
The mess we live in was created solely by you
You let things get so out of hand, things have to change
So you keep on fighting because you don't know what else to do!

Leaders of the Nations of the World
The people want change, we want peace
We want the world to get along, once and for all
We want all of this fighting and killing to cease!

Leaders of the Nations of the World
We want to be able to walk freely, just like days of old
We do not want to be discriminated because of our race or religion
We want our freedom back, not to be controlled!

Leaders of the Nations of the World
It is our born right to ask for this from you
Soon when people will realize, we are all created equal
Will you become a Nation to look up to?

Leaders of the Nations of the World
Religious leaders have pleaded with you time and time again
It's not too late to change your ways and make amends
Before you end up destroying us, all in the end!

Leaders of the Nations of the World
This world was created for people to live in Harmony and Peace
Do you all forget that God wants us to love one another?
Or are you going to set back while the world destroys itself,
Piece By Piece!

Thank You Lord For This Day....

Thank you Lord for giving me this beautiful day
I am so grateful for just being here today.
Every night I go to bed, wondering if it will be my last
Every morning at dawn, I smile to see the night has past.
I love life and all it has to offer, my family and friends
But I know there is so much waiting for me, when it finally ends.
I love to watch the dawn of day, when the sun arises
The night sky lights blink back and forth, full of many surprises.
I love the little creeks and rivers that flow to the mighty seas
I also love the howl of the cold north wind, as well as the soft summer breeze.
I love to watch the first snow as it falls slowly to the ground
But I also love the first spring flowers, waiting to be found.

Linda Laybolt
Whispers From Heaven

I love to listen to the little birds in the trees as they sing
Priceless is the joy and happiness to my heart that they bring.
I love to listen to the rain as it falls on my roof outside
But thunder and lightning, I'm sorry Lord, I'd rather be inside.
I love your colorful rainbows as they stretch across the sky
But I also love your beautiful, majestic mountains, sitting up so high.
I love to listen to the waves and the sounds that they make
I love to see them hit the shore, just before they break.
Each day that you give me is a new beginning of love
Perfection at its best, created by you, My Father in Heaven above!
So once again, I thank you Lord from the bottom of my heart
For this new precious day as it begins to start!

My Angel Is Home

Linda Laybolt
Whispers From Heaven

As He held her close, next to Him
The little baby was full of delight
She seemed to be so contented now
Everything was going to be alright!

He looked at her and gave her a kiss
You are so sweet, My Dear Little Child
Eyes of blue, with bright rosy cheeks
My little angel, meek and mild!

You had a rough go of it
Down there on earth
You never got to enjoy life
Since your premature birth!

Your parents wanted and loved you
But life for you was not meant to be
You held on for awhile, but deep down
You always knew, you would return to me!

All is not lost, My Dear Little One
You left behind, a legacy of love
Welcome Back, My Dear Little Angel
To Your Home With Me, In Heaven Above!

Collection Of Stories

The Christmas Angel

This is a story about a little angel who wanted to sit on top of a Christmas tree
So she went to God to ask him if she could sit on a tree for all to see
She pleaded, up on a tree, I'll shine so bright
If you will let me go on a tree, Christmas Night.

God looked at her and quietly asked, Why dear one would you want to shine on a tree?
When you shine so brightly up here in heaven for me
The angel replied, I just want to take some love from up here to there
So the children will see that we are real and do care.

Alright little one, I'll let you go
For your heart is full of love, that I know
But remember, it's not going to be as easy as you think it will be
Christmas Day you will return home here with me.

All of a sudden, it got real dark and cold
The little angel could not move, so the story is told
For there she lay in a box full of Christmas ornaments, completely out of sight
Not on a tree shining beautiful and bright.

I'm not suppose to be in here packed away
I'm suppose to be on a tree shining my love, she did say
The ornaments all started laughing hysterically, making fun of the little one
It's been years since anyone even looked at us, for our work is all done.

But I'm an angel from heaven. the little one said
Ha, ha ,ha replied the ornaments, you're old and dusty and can't even turn your head
Why all of a sudden, do you think you should shine
We've been packed away for years now and we're doing just fine.

Linda Laybolt
Whispers From Heaven

Suddenly some people came in to where the little angel lay
As she listened, she heard one of them say, decorations we need for the big day
The little angel started grinning from ear to ear
As she could hear them picking up boxes, ever so near.

The ornaments started laughing saying, we're not going anywhere
Do you really think that we'll get out of here?
Wipe that silly grin from your face, you silly old thing
Long forgotten you are, with that broken old wing.

Will you please stop laughing and making fun of me that way
You obviously don't listen to a word I say
I'm an angel sent from heaven that will shine so bright
I'll be giving out love in my light on that tree Christmas night.

In this box for many years, we abide
In case you don't get it, we've been tossed aside
You're an angel alright, you're an ornament just like us
So be quiet now and stop making a fuss!

Take us and open us , open us please
The little angel shouted, put us on that big Christmas tree
Then, all the ornaments took to great laughter, they can't hear you
Laughing harder, saying what is the angel from heaven going to do?

As they all laughed, the little angels eyes filled with tears
I want on that tree, she sobbed but none of you cares
There really wasn't anything she could do so she started to sing
Put me on top of that tree for much love to all I will bring!

Just then someone picked up the old dusty box where they all lay
Saying these are old and for years they have been hidden away
I'm taking them out to take a look and see
If they are good enough to go on our tree!

Linda Laybolt
Whispers From Heaven

Before they knew it, she had them all on display
As she carefully picked them up, she said they are all ok
Hmmm, I'm not sure if I can fix the angel's wing but I will do my best
As for the others, we'll clean them up and hang on the tree with all the rest!

The little angel never said a word , the smile on her face said it all
The others squawked about getting cleaned while she just sit hoping not to fall
The woman carefully glued her wing back on
That's when the angel started again to sing her song!

She took them one by one placing them all on the tree
The little angel was placed on last with a new light in her for all to see
Smiling and singing, she shouted this is the place where I am supposed to be
Proudly sitting on top of this big Christmas Tree!

The next night being Christmas Eve, all the lights were brightly lit
Which made everyone at church more full of the holiday spirit
And when the little angels light was plugged in
Everyone felt the love from her light go to their heart deep within!

The more songs about the birth of Baby Jesus that they did sing
The more love from her, to them she did bring
She could see God smiling and saying to her from heaven above
My dear little one, you are so right, the true meaning of Christmas is all about love!

Linda Laybolt
Whispers From Heaven

The Forgotten Gift

A Story:

The little boy awakened jumping with joy
At last, it was Christmas Day today
His voice echoed throughout the house
Get Up! Get Up! It's Christmas Day!

Smiling and laughing, he jumped out of bed
Down the stairs, he quickly fled
He stopped to see if the milk and cookies were gone
That he had left for Santa to snack on!

His face was glowing, when he reached the tree
Piles of presents, was all he could see!
He looked under the tree with a sad look of despair
The only gift he wanted, definitely was not there!

His parents could see the tears in his eyes
Which to them was quite a surprise!
He told them to call Santa, to come back
And to take all the stuff, back home in his sack!

Upon announcing this, he ran to his room
Christmas was suppose to be happy, not full of gloom!
When he reached his room, he jumped in his bed
Then, he pulled the blankets over his head!

Both parents were in complete shock
Everything he had asked for was in his sock!
They could not understand why he was so upset
What was it that Santa had forgot to get?

Up the stairs, both of them went
To see what was the most wanted, forgotten present!
When they reached his room, they could hear his cries
So they went in, to dry the tears from his eyes!

Linda Laybolt
Whispers From Heaven

The little boy reached out, to cling to his mother
The parents glanced back and forth, at each other!
The little boy started to tell them
The only thing that he wanted, that was not left for him!

Today is very big day, it's Christmas Day
I wanted to wish Jesus myself...."Happy Birthday!"
Santa was suppose to bring Him to me
He was suppose to be here this morning, under the tree!

That's all I asked Santa to bring
I never asked for another thing!
Now, Jesus will be mad and not love me
Because Santa forgot to put Him, under the tree!

I have a special gift for Jesus
I made it at kindergarden for Him, from all of us!
Now, He will never know
How much I love Him so!

Both parents could not believe
That this was the gift Santa forgot to leave!
Jesus still loves you, they both said
Now it's time for you to get, out of bed!

They all proceeded to get dressed and ready
As they were running late already!
The Christmas Service was held at exactly ten
Every year, over and over again!

They told their son to take along, the present
And off to church, the three of them went.
The little boy looked all around
But no sign of Jesus was to be found!

Inside the church, they could hear the bells ring
Away in a Manager, the congretation started to sing!
The little boy told his mother, I have to go pee
You don't have to come with me!

Linda Laybolt
Whispers From Heaven

He slowly made his way to the door that led outside
Over to the huge Nativity, he walked with pride!
He pulled out his wrapped present, placing it beside Baby Jesus
This is not much he said, but it's from all of us!

I wanted to give it to you, in person today
Because it's Christmas and Your Birthday!
Tears in his eyes, he said...I made it especially for you
Because Jesus, I love you!

As he started walking away, he heard a voice say "Wait!"
You can give it to me, it's not to late!
When he turned around, Jesus was standing there
Opening the present, with great care!

Smiling, inside the box was a star with a note
Jesus read out loud, what was wrote!
My teacher wrote this for me, to give to you
Happy Birthday Jesus, I love you!

Jesus wrapped His arms around the little boy
He said, "Thank You, for giving me so much Joy!"
Always Remember, I will always love you!
No matter what happens, I'll never be mad at you!

The little boy went back in the church and sat down
All you could see now was a big smile, not one frown!
When they got home, he rushed to the tree
And yelled; "Thank You, Santa for bringing Jesus to me!"

Janie's Christmas Gift

Note: This is very long but I hope you will take the time to read it.
Thanks....Linda

As I glanced out my kitchen window, I noticed
The snow was gently falling upon the ground
Another lonely Christmas Eve again
For none of my friends had come round.

Turning on the television
I said how can this possibly be
Nothing on but Santa Clause and Church Choirs singing
Is that all there is to see?

So I got up, reached for my hat and put my coat on
And decided to go, for a long leisurely walk
Maybe I will see someone who will talk to me
But I started to get tired, fourth time round the block.

All the houses were lit up with colorful lights and decorations
I could see passing by, their Christmas trees shining brightly inside
People were smiling, laughing, having so much fun
While I felt so lonely, standing alone in the cold outside.

I said to myself, enough of this I'm going home
I can't take anymore of this so-called holiday cheer
As I headed for home, I quickly turned around
A little girls voice off in a distance, I faintly did hear.

Slowly as I walked back down the street
The voice seemed to get louder, with each step that I made
I found her standing on church steps, saying please let me in
She was about five, with a big white smile, which she proudly displayed.

Linda Laybolt
Whispers From Heaven

Are you a friend of God's because this is his house?
No, I replied seeing the sadness in her face
Well sir, will you let me in so I can talk to him
I have something to give him that I brought from my place.

Not knowing what I should do, I decided to open the door
And let the little one go inside, out of the cold
She sat down on a pew and curiously looked around
Then she took a napkin out of her pocket, placing it her hand to hold.

Where are your parents? They must be worried about you
Shouldn't you be home getting ready for Santa as its Christmas Eve tonight
She looked up at me, with tears running from her eyes
I have to speak to God tonight, I promise to be real good and polite.

Thinking to myself, this childs parents must be full of worry
I asked what her name was and if she knew where she did live
She replied very lowly that her name was Janie
Then announced, I am not leaving, for God I have something to give.

She had long blond curly hair that went half way down her back
When she smiled, her face seemed to glow
I noticed her dark blue dress looked like it was something made from years ago
And here she sat diligently beside me, waiting for God to show.

For a couple of hours we sat there, as she casually talked to me
Mostly about Christmas, and the angels who lived in heaven above
Nothing at all about Santa Clause and his reindeers
Only about the angels whom she said, were so full of God's love.

I thought to myself, how does this little child know so much
While I seem to know so little on the topics, she's so innocently speaking of
But then I started to think about it
What does a child really know about love?

Linda Laybolt
Whispers From Heaven

Do you know God, sir?
No dear, I solemnly said
Feeling somewhat guilty all of a sudden
I fastly changed the subject with, you got to go home now and get ready for bed.

I'll go, she replied with a mighty big yawn
But you have to promise to give this to God for me
She passed me the napkin, she held so tightly in her little hand
There is something in there, I want God to see.

I know its not much but Momma says its the thought that counts
Tomorrow is the day Baby Jesus was born, I really don't want to leave
Would you kindly hold on to this and give it to God for him
For Momma says its better to give, than it is to receive.

She watched as I placed the white napkin into my pocket with care
When you see God, make sure you tell him its from me for his baby son
I shut off the lights as she scooted by me out the door
And when I came out, there was no sign of the little one.

I called out Janie at loud as I could yell
But there was no answer coming back from her
I must go to her house and see if she got home
A little girl alone at night put my heart in quite a big stir.

She had told me she lived over yonder on King Street
Which was very close and not far away
When I found the house and rang the doorbell
It occured to me, just exactly, what was I going to say?

An elderly man about eighty years old appeared at the door
I knew there and then, this was the wrong house, I came to
Smiling at me with a big grin from ear to ear
He said, Come in, we've been patiently waiting for you.

Linda Laybolt
Whispers From Heaven

I tried to tell the old man, I had made a mistake
But he abrupty turned, walking away waving me to come in
As he led me through his house to his sitting room
A feeling of love and warmth filled my heart within.

As I looked around, not knowing what to say
I could see lights shining on a well decorated tree
Angels of every kind lay hanging on its branches
While one big one full of lights sat proudly on the top for all to see.

A little old woman walked through the door handing me a very hot cup of tea
Christmas Eve, for some people can be a very lonely time of the year
We are so happy you could come here and spend the evening with us
And as she turned to sit down, I'm positive I saw in her eye, a great big humongous tear.

As I comfortably sat there, I completely forgot the reason why I was here
I listened with ease, taking in every word that the old folks had to say
On the fireplace mantle, only one Christmas stocking hung
And beside it , to my shock, Janie in her dark blue little dress, her picture did lay.

I knew then I was at the right house and wondered if she was ok
So I asked the old folks was their grand-daughter Janie safely tucked in bed
All of a sudden, they both stopped talking, their voices became very low
That is not our granddaughter, its our daughter, Janie, who now lives in heaven, they calmly said.

I could feel a lump forming in my throat , as my eyes filled quickly with tears
I am so sorry for asking you, something so very wrong
It's quite alright, how could you know as they placed their arms around me
Many Christmas's have passed, since our little Janie has been gone.

Linda Laybolt
Whispers From Heaven

Then the old folks sat back in their seats ,speaking of their sweet little girl
She dearly loved Christmas and giving gifts, what more can we say
She always said she wanted to be an angel, and carried a little metal one in her pocket
Tha'ts why our house is so full of angels, her memory lives on, each and every day.

We know that you have seen her, otherwise, here, you would not be
Every Christmas Eve, she lets us know that in her heart, we are there
We are never alone on this holy night, because here a always knock comes to our door
Just like you, she sends someone to us, who needs some tender loving care.

As I got up to leave, I felt like this had been the best night of my life
I know, for sure, it was the best Christmas Eve, I have ever had
As I hugged the old folks, giving them each a big kiss goodbye
I did not feel lonely anymore but somehow, I felt a little bit sad.

On the way home, I thought what a fool I have been
Never seeing Christmas for what it really is all this time
Tomorrow, I am changing my ways, for I want to learn more about God
I want this feeling of love to stay and forever be mine.

When I finally reached home, it was getting quite late
I thought about the old folks, whom God truly did bless
But I had the greatest blessing of all, when I unfolded Janie's napkin
A small metal angel with blond hair was smiling at me, in her dark, blue, little dress.

Christmas At Home

Softly rocking back and forth patiently waiting
The old lady sat peacefully knitting in her wooden rocking chair
Shadows of heat bounce on the wall, from her wood stove
Now and again, the oil lamp flickers, causing the wick to flare.

Outside the north wind was howling making itself known
Her lane way was filled with drifts of never ending snow
All alone on Christmas Eve but somehow, this year seemed different
With the roads all covered in snow, it was impossible for people to come and go.

I feel so lonely, it's not the end of the world
My family will get here sometime as she shed a little tear
I'm nice and warm in here and really, that's all that matters
Perhaps, they will be all here for Christmas Day next year.

Suddenly, she heard a loud bang on her door from her front porch
She thought, Who would be out in this storm and come to my place ?
As she opened the door, a man and woman solemnly stood there
Looking near froze all covered in snow from their feet up to their face.

Our car is broke down and we saw your light off in a distance
Please come right in and get warm, the old lady said
Take off your coats and sit over by the wood stove
I'll give you some hot tea along with some Christmas bread.

I can't believe my eyes that I am seeing someone tonight
My family was suppose to come and spend Christmas with me
But because of the storm no one will get anywhere
So make yourself at home, for here awhile, you are going to be.

They told the old lady that they were on their way to visit family
They knew there was going to be a winter storm but did not know how bad
It was going to be a surprise so no one knows we are coming
Glancing at each other, the man said," Christmas without family can be so sad."

Linda Laybolt
Whispers From Heaven

I have been baking now for weeks on end
I have a big turkey all ready to go in the oven tomorrow morning
My tree is all decorated with lights and full of ornaments
I was already for my family but the storm came up without any warning.

The old lady smiled at them, don't worry and don't look so sad
For this year, I'm going to make you both my family
We will have Christmas just like it was always meant to be
I am so happy in this storm, just to have some company!

They sat up for hours talking and laughing where it was so cosy inside
While the snow kept falling, the wind kept howling outside
Before they knew it, it was way past midnight
The old lady said, it's time for bed, for me this is a real late night.

She led them upstairs and showed them to their room
She handed them an extra quilt for their bed
Then she bid them both good night and pleasant dreams
With a smile on her face, off to bed she quietly fled.

Next day as they prepared to eat Christmas dinner
The woman asked the old lady did she wish her kids could be here
She looked at her with tears in her eyes and started to quietly sob
I have something to tell you, it's something for years that I have had to endear.

My family are not coming home this or any other year
Christmas Eve years ago, they had a fateful accident on their way home
Every year I get prepared for Christmas, waiting for them to show
I've done it for years, not because I am foolish, I am just so lonesome.

Many snow storms have come and gone since that Christmas Day
The old lady never spent another Christmas alone
We come up here every Christmas Eve and spend the holidays with her
Because as the old saying goes, There's just no place like home!

Run Free, My Beautiful Unicorn!

Nestled in the depths of the forest, a young stallion was born
His fur was white as snow, as well as his extra long mane
He completely resembled his parents, who were the last two left
Remaining in the once secluded, land of unicorn domain!

The others had left a few months before, but they had decided to stay
They both wanted their little foal born here, in the valley of their home
Once it was a safe environment, where the unicorns dwelled without fear
Then humans invaded, making it impossible for them to freely roam!

They named their young stallion Freedom, a name that brought hope
They would follow the others, when he was much bigger and stronger
They had been given a new land, full of green pastures and meadows
A land far away with freedom to roam, without fear any longer!

As the days passed, Freedom was growing at a fast rate
His parents watched over him, never letting him get to far out of sight
They told him many stories about his ancestors, and their great protector
Who was coming to take them Home, when the time was just right!

They spoke of when he would grow up huge and strong, just like his father
They called him, their little Prince, whom they loved and adored
Many hours of the day were spent giving praise and thanks
To their great Protector and Creator of all living things, their Loving Lord!

The unicorns held beauty, beyond all others in the forest
God gave them much wisdom, the unicorns were truly made out of love
When he saw that their species was being hunted by man
He decided to take them to a safe place, His Home in Heaven Above!

Linda Laybolt
Whispers From Heaven

One day while his mother was sleeping, Freedom decided to go exploring
His father had left earlier that day, to gather food in a pasture nearby
When he returned, there was no sign of Freedom anywhere
Both parents panicked, the search was on hoping to hear Freedom's cry!

Just as they got outside the valley, they heard voices
Human voices shouted, "There he is, Let's get him!"
Realizing the humans were after them, they turned to run
But ran right into a trap, that captured the both of them!

They put ropes on both the parents, which made it impossible to escape
They led them through the forests, laughing proudly at the unicorns
Capturing you means great rewards for us from our King
Wait till everyone sees you and those great mighty horns!

The parents were upset for letting themselves get captured
But they were more concerned about their little Prince Freedom
How would he survive alone in the forests without them
He was too young to be alone, without his parents love and wisdom!

Realizing that they may never see their little foal again, the parents cried out
Please, take care of our little baby, please protect him!
The parents had called upon their protector, their Lord in Heaven
Keep him safe from all harm, not a word about rescuing them!

Finally, after travelling for hours, the humans stopped for the night
They tied the unicorns to their horses and also to a tree
There was no way either could escape, which made them worried and sad
Reluctantly they settled down, the first time in their life, not being free!

Linda Laybolt
Whispers From Heaven

Half way through the night, they heard a sound that woke them up
Standing beside them were two angels, that quietly untied the pair
All of a sudden, both the unicorns had big white beautiful wings
When they flapped them, both were lifted high up in the air!

Within minutes, they were in new surroundings, their new Home
The Lord had heard their cries unto Him and had set them free
But there was no sight of Freedom, anywhere to be found
Their precious little baby, "Where, Oh Where could he be?"

Meanwhile back on earth, Freedom was having the time of his life
In the meadows, he had met and made some new friends to play with
They had to be unicorns too, but they were black in color
He wondered, unicorns are supposed to be white, maybe thats a myth!

Freedom decided he better go home, saying he'd come back again to play
When he reached home, there was no sign of his mother anywhere
He called out to her but no answer, so he called his father
Father would hear his voice floating through the air!

It was starting to get dark now, Freedom was really scared
Where are my parents, where did they go?, he cried!
Then, he heard a male voice say Little one, What is wrong?
Before he knew it, a huge black stallion was standing, by his side!

When Freedom explained to the stallion, that his parents were missing
The old stallion replied, Come with me, I'll take you to my place!
Freedom was debating whether to go or not, but decided he better
After all, this stallion was definitely one of his race!

Everyday, Freedom returned to the valley but still no sign of his parents
Then unto the meadows, he trotted at full speed to see his friend
He looked in every direction along the way, calling out to his parents
But still no sign of them was to be seen, time and time again!

Linda Laybolt
Whispers From Heaven

The days soon turned into months, Freedom was a fine young stallion now
The old stallion that took care of him was the leader of the herd
The old stallion knew that Freedom was a unicorn, not like the rest
He figured that his parents had been caught, but he said not a word!

Freedom had learned to love the old stallion, but still missed his parents
But he could not figure out why, they had left him all alone
Freedom was so grateful to the old stallion, for looking after him
The old stallion loved Freedom and thought of him as one of his own!

Freedom had always told his friends that he was a prince
But his friends laughed and teased him, A Prince Indeed, they would say
Princes don't have long white hair or that long horn in front of their head
Princes are handsome and strong, they don't have time to run and play!

But Freedom was indeed handsome and strong, and very smart
His only problem was that he still missed his loving parents, so much
Even though, he was a fine young stallion,all grown-up
He still missed the warmth of his parents loving touch!

He still went to the valley everyday and called for his parents
But this one day, something was different in the air
He kept on thinking about what his Mother had said
About the protector being his Lord and always there!

So he looked up to the sky and shouted at the top of his lungs
Protector, Oh Great Protector, Are you there?
Please, come and take me to my new home, to be with my parents
Protector, My Lord, please hear my prayer!

Freedom started to cry, Why protector, do you not come for me?
Why did you not take me home and leave me here all alone?
Just then, a bright light appeared in the sky above Freedom
A soft voice spoke saying Freedom, you have never been on your own!

I led you to the old stallion, who took good care of you
His family welcome you, loved you as part of theirs
I have watched you grow from a small foal, to a beautiful stallion
I have always been here by your side, in good and despair!

Your parents wanted you to grow to love the land, in which you were born
I have waited years for you to raise up your voice unto me
I have waited for you to call me, to take you Home, My Dear Prince
All you had to do was ask, and I would have come to thee!

Freedom felt so much love go into his heart, he had finally met his Creator
Lord, he asked, Will my parents be there waiting for me?
Yes, he replied. They are going to be amazed when they see you!
Come, Freedom; It's time to go and be as all Unicorns are meant to be,
"Home, Running Free!"

When God Created Angels For The Earth

A Story:

One day God decided that, He was going to create angels
But Lord, you already have angels everywhere!
Gabriel wondered, as he Himself was an Archangel
God replied, Not for here but for earth, down there!

This struck Gabriel as odd since earth already had angels
There are many angels watching and protecting the earth!
Why do you want to create more to send there?
God smiled at Gabriel, These angels will experience human birth!

Linda Laybolt
Whispers From Heaven

Come Gabriel, I have some thinking to do, God declared!
These angels have to be my very best, that I have ever made!
Gabriel thought to himself, Oh My! What will become of me?
Unknown what the future held for him, he was abit afraid!

Then, God sat and thought for a long time
He looked at Gabriel, I want them to be like the angels here!
But when they are born, they will forget they are angels
In human form, many hardships they will endear!

Gabriel looked at God in shock! If they forget they are angels,
What good are they going to do and how can they be the best?
God smiled, they will possess all the qualities of angels and humans
They will carry my love in their heart, by me they will be blessed!

Hmmmm! thought Gabriel, this is going to be a tough one
Angels and humans are completely different, how can this be?
God smiled again at Gabriel, don't forget God knows all thoughts
I forgot to add Gabriel, they will also be like me!

They will have love for all people, no matter who they are
They will help any one, any time, any place
They will give comfort and compassion, when needed
They will be my secret messengers, full of love and grace!

They will know when to give a smile, to brighten someone's day
They will tend to the sick and needy, just because they want to
They will give comfort to the lonely, the elderly and the young
No one will be forgotten by them, their love will shine in all they do!

They will be like other humans, facing many trials and tribulations
But the love I place in their hearts, will overcome anything they face
They will have a strong love for me and never question it or me
My earth angels will be part of me, and All I will strongly embrace!

Linda Laybolt
Whispers From Heaven

Some will be born into life of riches, while others will be poor
Some will be live a long life, while others will not
Some will carry torches of hurt, others will be quite happy
But they all will carry in their hearts, a warm, loving, soft spot!

Gabriel was quite impressed with God, now full of great ease
These new angels were going to be Full of God's love, just like me
He felt ashamed for thinking the way he had
God's new angels would be the best, in every possible decree!

God said, it is time to send my new angels down to earth
Each one is ready, full of devotion and love
And unto the earth, they watched birth after birth
As the angels were sent down from Heaven Above!

As each angel was born into human form, God smiled
He still watches and smiles as they are born, to this very day
I know in my heart, that you are one of those Blessed Angels,
My Dear Friend, that God has sent Full of Love, To Come My Way!

Merry Christmas Mama

A Story:

As she looked down into his face,
she could see his eyes filling with tears.
It broke her heart to tell her little son,
there would be no Christmas this year.

It was a constant struggle fo her
since her husband had passed away.
There was no money for treats or even one toy,
for her little son on Christmas Day!

Although she had no joy in her heart,
her son had talked her into putting up a tree.
Looking at it made her heart ache and long,
for the way Christmas once used to be.

Linda Laybolt
Whispers From Heaven

With no one to help her work her fields,
she barely had enough grain and hay.
Between the barn work and her garden,
she was kept busy most of the day.

She had no family here to help her out,
most lived faraway in another state.
This was her husband's family farm,
her beloved soul-mate.

Most folks around here were farmers,
also struggling from day to day.
There was no one she could turn to for help,
sadness filled her heart, in a big way!

Tonight was the annual Christmas concert,
held at the church, in the local town.
She had promised to take her son,
who was full of excitement, jumping up and down.

Just about all her neighbours were there
Everyone was full of laughter and cheer.
Her son was having the time of his life,
while she was crying inside, in pain and despair.

At least, this outing was a small ray of happiness,
she could give her son tonight.
The smiles on his face said it all,
when he saw all the Christmas lights.

The concert lasted about an hour,
afterwards, there was lots of food to eat
Christmas carols were sung by all,
while the children snacked on, home-made treats.

When the two of them returned home,
it was very late, but her son was wide awake.
He was still going on to her about all the food,
he had ate, especially the Christmas Cake!

Linda Laybolt
Whispers From Heaven

As they stood on their porch, looking at the stars
He held her hand, saying Mama, thank you!
This was the best Christmas present ever,
Tonight you smiled and laughed,
Merry Christmas Mama, I love you!

Mark 12:13
And you shall love the Lord your God with all your heart and with all your soul and with all your mind and with all your strength.

The Angel Who Begged For Bread

.A Story:

The old man was known as the beggar in the town
People would stare and laugh, whenever he was around!
He had been born and raised in these parts, it is said
Everyone that passed by him, he begged for a piece of bread!

He wore the same old clothes all the time, and the same dirty hat
His pants were full of holes, his hair full of mats!
Seen only during the light of day, he was always friendly and polite
But once evening approached, he was long gone and out of sight!

Everyday, he would hobble over to his corner on the street
There he would greet everyone, then beg for something to eat!
He never asked for money, most folks in this town had none
This was the old west, cowboys, horses, and fancy guns!

The town's population was about four hundred, give or take
Big for this part of the country, without any mistake!
The town had a big store, where all goods were bought
From the outskirts farmers, wives and ranch hands came into town alot!

Linda Laybolt
Whispers From Heaven

The town had two saloons, the sherriff's office, one bank for all
A small bakery, a restaurant, a school, a church and one big horse stall!
On the outside of town, stood a big, run-down old place
Alone and forgotten, its small inhabitants were the towns disgrace!

This was the old orphanage, which had been built a few years ago
A place for all orphans who had no family, to go
Many babies born out of wedlock were left, here in shame
At the door by night bundled up, without a family name!

In the beginning when it was built, the town took care of it
But the babies kept increasing in population, bit by bit!
With so few adoptions, the town finally decided to close its door
Children who remained, the town no longer provided for!

Even the workers, who had been parents to these children
Left them to fend for themselves, alone and forsaken!
Some food and seeds was dropped off by farmers, once in awhile
Which gave the children some hope and a reason to smile!

Everyday, the ole man gathered bread and placed it in a sack
When his sack was full he would leave, carrying it on his back!
The town people would give him loaves upon loaves each day
But were curious about his whereabouts, when he went away!

One day the baker asked him, what do you do with all the bread?
The ole man looked up smiling, I am an angel, he said!
The baker laughed out loud, you sure don't look like an angel to me
Angels are beautiful! An ole man in rags is all that I see!

The baker left, returning to his shop shaking his head
Every morning, he gave the ole man his left over bread!
Tonight, I am going to follow the ole man to see where he goes
A question asked by all in town, for nobody knows!

Linda Laybolt
Whispers From Heaven

The baker watched all day for the ole man to leave
Finally, he packed up his sack in the early eve!
The baker stayed way back from the ole man as he made his way
Tonight, I will find out where the ole man stays!

Out of the town, the ole man slowly walked
With every step, the baker listened as the ole man talked!
He could not make out exactly what he was saying
Although it sounded as if the ole man was praying!

When the ole man reached his destination, he turned his head
His eyes focused on the baker, Come in, he said!
The baker stepped forward in shock, it was now all clear
This was the old orphanage, his eye shed a tear!

The ole man opened the door, six little ones appeared in sight
I bought a guest home with me, now please all be polite!
This is the baker, whom I have spoken to you all about
With his generous donation of bread everyday, you don't do without!

The baker looked at the six smiling faces that all said,
Thank you, Sir! For the bread that we are all fed!
The baker thought to himself, they are so charming and polite
They made him feel so special, which gave him delight!

The baker looked at the ole man, feeling full of shame
The ole man introduced the children, name after name!
Who looks after you all, when the ole man is in town?
One child spoke up, Why, the angels! They are always around!

The baker could not believe the words of the innocent child
He just looked at her and continued to smile!
The little girl said, David is an angel too, you know
She looked at the ole man, who now started to glow!

Suddenly, he was transformed into a beautiful male angel with wings
He was not the ole raggedy man anymore, but looked like a king!
He looked at the baker and put out his hand
You have now met an angel, he said Firsthand!

He explained to the baker, the children were left alone
They were too small to be left on their own!
God had sent the angels to them, to take care of
None of Gods children, should be left alone and unloved!

The baker went back to town that night
There has to be something I can do, to make this wrong right!
The next morning he gave the ole man a sack full of fresh bread
From his shop, word of the children needing homes, became widespread!

Within a month, all the children had loving homes to go to
The baker told the story about the angels to very few!
He knew that not many would believe or understand
That an angel from God was dressed as a beggar, in the form of a little ole man!
Would you?

Mark 12:13
And you shall love the Lord your God with all your heart and with all your soul and with all your mind and with all your strength.

Linda Laybolt
Whispers From Heaven

Do You Believe In Magic?

A Story:

Home, I thought, the hospital is her home, how tragic!
Then she looked at me and asked, do you believe in magic?

I was at the hospital waiting for X-rays somewhat, in distraught
When I saw a little girl sitting in a wheelchair, in deep thought!
It was no problem conceiving, that she was very ill
All the tubes coming from, her gave me a cold chill!
As she looked around studying the room, being good as gold
It dawned on me that she was all alone, approximately four years old!
Why would anyone leave this sick little girl all alone?
Thoughts kept racing through my mind, looks like she is on her own!
I looked at her in pity, such a sweet child
And then she looked over at me and smiled.
Hello! she said, as she turned her frail little body towards me
You're waiting for x-rays too, I see!
I replied yes, my dear, My Name is Sue
Now tell me little one, who are you?
Hi Sue, she announced, my name is Anne!
Then she put out her little hand.
Don't be afraid, I will not bite
Meeting you is such a delight!
I guess you can tell that I am not feeling so good
I would love to get up and run around, if I could!
My friends tell me, I was always on the go
Now I can hardly walk, and if I do, I am real slow!
I said to her, where is your Mama at, dear?
Hoping she would reply that she was somewhere near!
Mama is gone away, but not for good, this I know
She left me when I was a baby but I still love her, even so!
I never really knew her but I wished that I did
It's not easy not having a Mama, when you're a kid!
I thought to myself, what kind of mother leaves a sick child?
Just the thoughts of it, was getting me riled!
I said to her, where do you live and with whom?
She replied, why here at the hospital, I have a room!

Linda Laybolt
Whispers From Heaven

Does anyone come to visit with you?
Sometimes, the minister or workers stop by, but only a few!
She said, life isn't all that bad
Some days are good, while others are bad!
Don't feel sorry for me, I like it in this place
It's my home as she spoke with a smile on her face!
Home, I thought, the hospital is her home, how tragic!
Then she looked at me and asked, do you believe in magic?
Not really, I answered, do you?
Well of course, she said with a huge smile. I do!
Then I asked the foolish question, what kind of magic do you believe in?
All kinds, why every kind, she answered with a big grin!
Then she started to tell me the story of her life as she knew it
At four years old, I thought, this will only take a little bit!
Oh my, was I ever wrong, indeed I was wrong!
What this little girl was about to tell me, was extremely long!
She started out with I was born here to earth four years ago
They say you are not suppose to remember, but I sure do so!
Mama was singing to me as she was driving her car to the store
When all of a sudden, I heard a big roar!
I was still in Mama's belly then but I was tossed all around
There was a big crash and then there was no sound!
I listened to see if I could hear Mama talk
But all I could hear was people shouting and a big knock!
Then some men came and took Mama away
And then I was born on that day!
I never heard Mama's voice again ever
I guess she left me that day forever!
My friends told me that one day, I would see her again
And that they would stay with me, until then!
Then after that, they sent me to live with some kin
And that is really where the magic begin!
Even though, I was just a baby, I understood
That they didn't want me, so I had to be good!
My friends would pick me up and hold me, when I would cry
And to this day, they do and still sing to me sweet lullabies!
When I took sick, my aunt said she did not want me anymore
That with me sick, I was just an added chore!

Linda Laybolt
Whispers From Heaven

So some people came and took me away
Now this is my home, and for now, I will stay!
They tell me that I will not get better, but that does not bother me
For soon, I will be like the dove bird and fly free!
Oh, my heart ached for this little girl, I wanted to cry
It was very difficult, to look her straight in the eye!
I guess she could feel that I was not at ease
She looked up at me and said, Don't feel sorry for me, please!
I know that there are a lot of things, I would like to do
But my friends tell me, I will, when I get to the place, that I am going to!
They say Mama is waiting and counting the days, you see
For us to be together, for she really misses and wants to be with me!
What kind of people would fill this childs head with such nonsense?
Telling a little girl, she is going to die, it just does not make any sense!
Then a nurse appeared out of no where to take the little one
I said to her, what room are you in? I'll come to see you, we'll have fun!
And then she was gone and I sat there reflecting on what she had said
Tears flowed from my eyes, thinking of her days that laid ahead!
When I got home, I called the hospital to inquire about Anne
The nurses told me that no kin was in since her sickness began!
I asked if it would be okay for me to come into visit her one day
She replied yes, she needs someone in a very heartfelt way!
So the next day, I got up bright and early and out shopping I went
I wanted to bring Anne the perfect present!
After wandering through a bunch of stores, I found a doll
She was holding a little kitten and had wings that were very small!
I picked her up some coloring books and crayons too
And a bunch of kids books for her to look through!
I will never forget that day, or the look of happiness on her face
It is something that my mind will never erase!
She said, no one ever brings me anything
I love it all but I really love the angel with wings!
My friends are all saying, she looks just like us
They are laughing at her cute little dress!
I looked at her and said there is no one here but you and I
My friends are all here, can you not see them fly!
No, I could not see her imaginary friends

Linda Laybolt
Whispers From Heaven

And I never mentioned them to her again!
My visits back and forth to see Anne were quite regular now
I went as often as time would allow!
I found out from the nurses, there was no hope for her at all
It was just a matter of time for little Anne, who was so small!
My heart cried for this dear little girl, she was so sweet
I prayed everyday for a miracle for her, that death she would defeat!
I could see her failing with each passing day
And each passing day, the more I would pray!
The last time, I saw her, she was in real bad pain
She whispered, Sue I have something to ask you again!
Dear, I said what is it? Can I get you something?
Can I have Magic, my little doll with the wings?
Immediately, I got up and put it beside her in the bed for her to see
She said, when I am gone, will you look after Magic for me?
I could hardly talk but I mumbled yes sweetheart, I will
She said, my friends are telling me before I leave, I have one dream to fulfill!
I said Dear what is the dream that is so important to you?
Then, she said I needed to believe the Magic was true!
And as she said this, her room was filled with lights shining so bright
Smiling at me, she said do you see my friends wings and dresses of white?
Her room was full of angels, some by her bed holding her hand
They say, its time to go now Sue, Mama is waiting for her Anne!
Tears flowed from my eyes as she said, I'll always love you Sue
And I kissed her on her little face, I whispered I'll always love you too!
It's been six years now since little Anne passed away
I think about her many times a day!
I know in my heart she is with her Mama in Heaven Above
She is probably flying around with her little wings, non-stop like a dove!
No more sickness or confined to a chair
Her spirit is finally free, as the love within her, floats throughout the air!
Magic sits on my bedroom dresser, when I look at her I sometimes grieve
Anne taught me a real lesson in life, Magic is something to truly believe!

Linda Laybolt
Whispers From Heaven

Mark 12:13
And you shall love the Lord your God with all your heart and with all your soul and with all your mind and with all your strength.

The Story Of Bethlehem

A Story:

On Christmas Eve in just about every house, candles and trees are brightly lit
Family and friends come together, full of the holiday spirit.
Lots of special home baked goodies, for all to eat
Many new Christmas memories will be made, for us to keep.
The hustle and bustle of getting ready, for this day
Has finally come to an end, we can happily say.
For some, it's just another day to sleep in
But for others it has deep meaning, from the heart within.
Years ago Christmas used to be somewhat simple, compared to nowadays
Somehow the true meaning of Christmas got lost, in so many ways.
You may say that's not true, we help out those who are in need
It's that time of the year so we gladly give, what we can indeed!
There are other months of the year besides December, you know
Or do you just wait for Christmas, for a little love to show?
Many of you will remember what it was like, when we were young
so many Christmas concerts and all the carols, that were sung.
Giving Christmas greetings of Merry Christmas to everyone, that was in sight
Smiling and laughing as it gave our hearts, such joy and delight.
Receiving Christmas cards and parcels, with gifts in the mail
Always cheered our day, bringing a smile without fail.
Christmas Eve was sitting around the brightly lit Christmas tree
Hoping that Santa would put something, in the sock for me.
Grandma would bring us all a glass of home-made eggnog
While Dad checked the fire to see if it needed one more log.
Mom brought in some of her best cookies to share
And we all sat quietly as Grandpa settled in his wooden rocking chair.

Linda Laybolt
Whispers From Heaven

It was Grandpa's favorite time every year on Christmas Eve for him
All eyes and ears were focused as he began to tell, the story of Bethlehem.
He'd look at us all gathered around him, with a solemn look upon his face
His voice was deep but yet he spoke elegantly full of grace.
First, he would start off with "Never forget what I am about to tell you?"
It may not be word for word but it comes from the Holy Bible, which we all know is true.
An angel by the name of Gabriel appeared to a young woman one day
And told her to listen carefully to what he had to say.
Mary, you have been chosen by God to give birth to his son
He is the Messiah, sent from heaven, he is the chosen one.
Mary knew exactly what Gabriel was talking about
She would obey her God to the fullest, for the love she had for him was beyond any doubt.
Mary was a virgin who was going to wed Joseph, a carpenter by trade
I shall tell him of the plans, that our God has made.
Joseph was very reluctant at first but his love for Mary was one of a kind
After an angel appeared to him in a dream, he understood and it gave him much peace of mind.
When Mary was almost due to give birth, Joseph took her into Bethlehem
For he knew it would be safe there, for all of them.
Not a room could he find at an inn anywhere
The Son of God was on his way but no one seemed to care.
Finally, an inn keeper told them to go to his stall
It's the only thing I have to offer and it's almost nightfall.
So into the stall, they went out of the cold on this very night, many years ago
Tears would come into Grandpa's eyes about now and his voice would get very low.
It's so sad to think that the Son of God was born in what we call a barn today
He had no cradle to lay in, only a bed made out of straw and hay.
All the animals stood quietly and watched without blinking an eye
As Mary wrapped Baby Jesus in swaddles of cloth while outside a

bright star lit the whole sky.
Then, she lovingly kissed his little head
And laid him in a manger which was to be his bed.
Off in a far distance, heavenly hosts appeared to shepherds
announcing the arrival of the Messiah, God's only son
And many journeyed to see him bringing gifts, for they knew he was the chosen one.
The star that had lit in the sky led them all straight to Bethlehem
And in a manger in a stall is where they all humbly found him.
The angels sang Hallelujah, Glory be to the Father Most High, for Jesus,his son has come to the earth
For this is the night of our dear Saviour's birth.
Peace on earth, goodwill to all men
Forever, this day be remembered by all, Baby Jesus is born in Bethlehem!
Tears in his eyes, Grandpa would then look at all of us and say
As old as you get, may you never forget
The true meaning of Christmas Day!

The Last Leaf

A STORY:

The rustle of the branches bending back and forth
Swaying to the gentle wind, dancing with the breeze
Quietly singing with the rest of nature in tune
The leaves fluctuate, with great ease!

The heat of summer has ended, fall is here
Some major changes will be taking place
Cooler air soon will plunge onto all of nature
Not like the summer season, full of warmth and grace!

First, leaves will turn into vibrant colors
Displaying beauty proudly, unlike any other to be found
Their time for existence is at near end
Eventually, all will fall one by one to the ground!

Linda Laybolt
Whispers From Heaven

The leaves converse back and forth to each other
Talking about summer adventures, how much fun it has been
Saying good-bye to all their friends they hold dear
Giving last words of love to their offspring and kin!

One little leaf sits quietly, not saying a word
They can all fall to the ground, but here I will stay
Why Mama and Papa want to fall, I don't understand
That old north wind will not make me go away!

Slowly the leaves start to fall below to the cold ground
Everyone seems happy and so willing to go
Mama and Papa said they would see me again real soon
But I know this is lies and is just not so!

Soon the little leaf was all alone on the tree
Holding on was harder to do with each passing day
One day, the tree began to speak to the leaf
Go with your family, it's not right for you to stay!

But is I fall, I surely will die like the others
I want to live here forever, if you will let me
Go with your family, you will not die
Life awaits you down below, you will see!

But the little leaf refused to let go and hung on
The days were cold now, and he was to
He was so lonely and sad, and missed his family
So he let himself go and down through the air he flew!

Winter was long and cold, alot of snow had fell
Spring returned, little trees started to sprout everywhere
The little leaf opened his eyes, discovering he was alive
He heard his Mama and Papa shout, We're over here!

His Mama said, I told you I would see you again
But you would not listen and refused to fall
We are all trees now and will live for a long time
We will have many years together, because we are all small!

Linda Laybolt
Whispers From Heaven

The little tree said, Mama will I die someday and not come back?
Yes, his Mama replied but we will go to a much better place
High up in the sky is Heavens Garden, there we will all go
But till then, here we will stay in the warmth of God's Loving Grace!

Mark 12:13
And you shall love the Lord your God with all your heart and with all your soul and with all your mind and with all your strength.

Heaven's Garden Of Flowers

This is a story:

The little flower looked all around in amazement
Wow! she said as she laughed with joy
The sun is so bright but I am happy, I am alive!
Soon I will be in full bloom for all to enjoy!

Hello everyone, she excitedly announced
Two big flowers started to smile as they looked down at the little one
Hello to you, we are your parents
You finally are awake, must be from the light of the sun.

When will I bloom and be pretty like you? she asked
The parents laughter could be heard all around
It will not take long little one but first you have to grow
You will bloom when your stem comes way up from the ground.

The little flower loved sitting there with the other flowers
As soon as the sun would arise, they would open their eyes
Day after day, they told many stories to each other
And day after day, some of their friends, they said their good-byes.

The little flower looked up at her parents, where are they going to?
Do we all get to go someday too?
The parents replied, little one they are gone to Heaven's Garden
We will all go there and someday, you will too!

Linda Laybolt
Whispers From Heaven

What is heaven Mama? Is it a nice place?
Yes my darling little one, we all go there to the Lord's Garden when we die
Who is the Lord Mama? Is he nice?
Yes dear, he created you and loves you, she said with a sigh.

Why are we here then? Why aren't we in heaven?
We are here for the Lord to enjoy our beauty, we were made out of love
Soon, your father and I will go there but you must stay here
When the time is right, you will come be with us in the Lord's Garden in heaven above.

One day early in the morning, a man came walking where the flowers were
It is the Lord, little one don't make a sound
He walked up to the flowers and said what beauty you all have
I love all of you and then he continued to walk around.

The little one said to herself, I like him for he is very nice
We should all stay here forever and not go away
But unfortunately, this was the last time she would see her parents
We will see you in heaven's gardens little one for we leave today.

Days passed and the little was was getting bigger everyday
Before she knew it, she was an adult flower in full bloom
I love it here and I will never leave she declared to the others
But you will have no choice they said as winter will be here soon.

The days passed and the flower would not give in and leave
She shivered with the cold but held all her pedals close and tight
There she stood all alone for all the others had left one by one
And when morning came she would get warm by the suns light.

Linda Laybolt
Whispers From Heaven

The Lord appeared to her one day and smiled at her
What have we got here he said as he smiled at her from where he stood
Why won't you come to my warm garden in heaven with the others?
She replied, I want you to admire me, I thought that you understood!

The Lord started to grin from ear to ear
Everyday, I will admire you in my garden in heaven above
The little flower was jumping with joy when he picked her up from the ground
Because all she ever wanted was to be near him and feel the warmth of his neverending love!

Saddie And The Crow

A Story:

The little boy and girl were playing outside
Let's play hide and seek, I'll count, you go hide!
Off into the woods, the little girl ran as fast as she could
I've gotta find a place to hide, that is good!
Over yonder looks like a good place
He'll never find me here, she thought with a smile on her face!
She sat and waited for her friend, the search was on
This is taking too long, she started to yawn!
So she decided that she better let a shout out
As she started to take a walk about!
She carefully listened to the singing of the birds
When all of a sudden, she heard a string of words!
Hey you down there, what are you doing here?
She looked up and around but no one was there!
What's the matter, the cat got your tongue
You should not be alone out here, you're way to young!
The little girl was now a little bit scared and looked all around
Who is that talking she thought, trying not to make a sound!
The little girl started to run but a voice shouted, you cannot hide
Don't be afraid, I will not hurt you, the voice replied!
The little girl stopped and said where are you?
She felt something touch her shoulder, a small voice said, how do you

Linda Laybolt
Whispers From Heaven

do?
The little girl was scared to turn around and take a peek
What's the matter? she heard, you don't want to speak?
Then she felt something strange touch her cheek, with Hello! Hello!
Then, she saw it, on her shoulder sat a big black crow!
My name is George and what is yours young lady?
Shyly she answered with a smile on her face, I'm Saddie!
Well, hello Saddie, I am going to take you home
This is a big forest and in here, you should never roam!
Saddie looked at the bird, you can talk!
Well of course, I can talk replied George as if he was in shock!
I am an angel sent here to watch over you
Saddie started to laugh, you are no angel, that I know is true!
Angels are pretty and have big white wings you know
Well I have wings and can fly too, said the crow!
Saddie laughed some more, I know an angel when I see one
George answered, but how many have you seen, my guess is none!
George flapped his wings and started to fly
I am beautiful too like the angels and can fly way up in the sky!
You are an ugly old crow, laughed Saddie some more
You are wrong, I've seen pictures of angels before!
Ah, replied George but I bet you never seen any as pretty as me?
I can talk, I can fly, I am as pretty as can be!
Then George landed back on Saddie's shoulder, walk that way he said
And out of the forest, Saddie was lead!
When Saddie saw her house, she started to run fast
The walk had been long, she was home at last!
George was flying shouting, We're here! We're here!
He flew up beside Saddie saying, I will be watching you in her ear!
Saddie said to George, Please, don't leave and go away!
I will even call you an angel, if you will just stay!
Just then George turned into a beautiful angel and flew up in the air
I have always been with you, I am with you everywhere!
I am your guardian angel but I did not want to scare you
So I appeared as a crow, something you knew!
So go in your house now, but always remember, I am here
You may not see me, but from you, I will never disappear!
Then George turned back into a crow
As he flew away, he yelled to Saddie, I love you so!

Whispers From Heaven

The Treasure

A Story:

For years talk was all around the the village, about the old man's treasure
He himself bragged about how he kept it safe and secure!
Many tried to trick the old man into telling where it was hidden
But no matter what they said, the old man didn't!

No one knew how the treaure had come into his possession
Over the years, the treasure had become the villagers main obsession!
Everyone wanted it for the old man said, in it held all the riches of life
The only other person that had seen it, was his loyal wife!

Often he said, it was worth more than all the gold in the world combined
Just knowing that he had it gave him complete, peace of mind!
Although he lived on a farm, he claimed he was the riches man around
He constantly gave credit to His God in Heaven for the treasure, he had found!

Many tried to steal the treasure but could not find it
For years people would search his place many times, bit by bit!
When the old man's wife died all thought he would tell, where it was hid
But as the days of his life grew shorter, he never did!

When the old man finally passed away, the village people did not care
The only concern they had was the treasure, hidden somewhere!
After searching for days, they all decided that there was no treasure
And if there was, the old man took the hidden place to his grave, with him forever!

The old man had no family leaving everything he owned, to the local church
But all the congregation had been there too, helping with the search!
Everyone thought that they were all going to end up well to do
But now reality had hit, for this was far from being true!

Linda Laybolt
Whispers From Heaven

So they decided to clean out his house and get it ready to sell
After days of cleaning and packing, everything was going very well!
Then a woman picked up his old Bible that laid by his bed
And started to read what the ole man had written in the front of it in red!

My Holy Bible is my most precious treasure
It is worth more than all the world's gold of pleasure!
A rich man I will always be, when I open its fragile pages
And read the Lord's Words, that was written through time, over the ages!

Forever, I will give praise to My Lord for this treasure, he has given to me
In it is written all there is to know about life, and all eternity!
There are no riches on earth, that could ever compare to His Love
Someday, I will walk streets of gold with God, in His Mighty Kingdom, in Heaven Above!

After reading this, she read it to the villagers with tears in her eyes
She said the old man told the truth about his treasure, there was no lies!
So they placed the old man's Bible in the church on display
With a sign beside it saying, The Greatest Treasure on Earth Lays Here, Today And Always!

A Prayer Gets Answered.....

A Story:

Follow your heart wherever it may lead you
You never know where it may lead you....

A young girl named Kathy was riding a bike one day
She was so excited because today was her birthday.
She has finally turned ten years old

Linda Laybolt
Whispers From Heaven

The sun was shining but it was bitter cold.
She was out in the country on an old dirt road
She was looking at all the sights as she rode.
Suddenly, she heard a voice but could not see noone
So she decided to turn her bike around and run.
But as she slowed down, she heard a woman say
Don't be afraid and please don't go away!
She stopped and looked around again some more
Because the womans voice was kind of hard to ignore.
Finally, she saw her standing next to the trees
Leaning on a cane, the old lady made her feel quite unease.
She said, I see you almost everyday riding by here
So I thought I'd come and say hello to you dear.
My name is Abigail and I live all alone in a small house
The only friend I get to talk to is a little grey mouse.
Would you like to come and visit me someday?
I can tell you lots of stories, I have much to say.
Kathy smiled and said sure I'll drop in to see you
But right at the moment, I have something to do.
The next day a knock came to the old womans door
There stood the little girl from the day before.
Come in, my dear child from out of the cold
The beginning of a long friendship is about to unfold.
Abigail said she grew up in her house and always lived there
She had no family left living as she rocked back and forth in her chair.
All her neigbours had passed on or moved away
But she loved her home, so she decided to stay.
She told Abigail many stories about the past
She wanted their time together to go slowly but not fast.
Everyday the little girl showed up at her door
Abigail showed no signs of being lonely no more.
Everyday before Kathy left, she'd pull out a book
And read passages from it, without even taking a look.
She told Kathy, this book means so much to me
It's the greatest book ever written, I'm sure you'll agree!
I am getting very old now and my days are numbered I know
I prayed to God to see an angel, before it's my time to go.
Kathy smiled and gave Abigail a big hug and kiss on the cheek
Tears filled the old ladys eyes, she could hardly speak.

Linda Laybolt
Whispers From Heaven

She said I followed my heart and walked out to the road
And my prayers were answered by a little girl whose love overflowed.
I'll never be able to thank you enough for coming here each day
I'm so grateful to the Lord for answering my prayer everyday.
Kathy smiled and said I will be back tomorrow to visit you
I'll come everyday as long as you want me to.
When Kathy left, Abigail began to pray before she went to bed
She thanked the Lord again and again, while wiping the tears she shed.
Meanwhile, Kathy watched the old woman and started to sing
Praise to the Lord as she lifted herself up and spread open each wing!

One Way Ticket To Heaven

A Story:

The young boy looked all around the station
Trying to figure out which ticket booth to go to.
After reading all the destinations
He wasn't sure what to do.

He decided he better sit for awhile
He looked way too young to be travelling on his own.
Just from looking at his height, he may have been around six
Way too young to be in this big station all alone.

He carried a small backpack with a picture of spiderman
There did not look to be much packed inside
He looked kind of scared as he watched people walk by
Almost as if he were someone who had been cast aside.

Finally he got up and headed to the ticket booth
The sales clerk looked down at the little one.
May I buy a one way ticket to Heaven please?
I have to get there before this day is done!

Linda Laybolt
Whispers From Heaven

The sales clerk did not know what to say
No one had ever asked for a ticket to Heaven before.
She said aren't you too young to be travelling on your own?
The boy replied, please sell me the ticket, thats what I came here for.

I am very sorry but I cannot sell you the ticket you asked for
We don't travel to that destination, only to places close by.
Give me your home phone number and I will call your parents
They can come and get you if they live nearby.

The little boy looked up at the woman with tears in his eyes
My parents are not at home anymore, they are gone away.
Why would parents leave this small child on his own?
Something is not right here as she looked at the child in dismay.

She said, you stay right there and I will come out to you
Quickly she put her closed sign up and made her way out.
She took the little boy by his hand over to a seat to talk
He has to be a runaway she thought, beyond any doubt.

Tell me she asked, are things ok at home?
Do you feel that you have to leave to get away?
There are people that can help you, you know
Instead of being here. you should be out having fun today.

The little boy started to cry, I want my Mommy and Daddy
But I have to go to Heaven first, to see Jesus.
They went there to live with Jesus and His Angels
That's why I want to take the bus!

The clerk felt so overwhelmed by the little boys story
She started to cry along with the little boy too.
I have to make some phone calls she said
In the meantime, I promise I will take good care of you!

After she had got the little boys name she called the police
And yes there was a big search on trying to find this little one.
She was told to keep him there and they were on their way
You never know he may take off again on the run.

Linda Laybolt
Whispers From Heaven

When they came for the little boy, she was told he was all alone
He had no family and was a ward of the childrens aide.
She asked when his parents had died
They replied two days ago, this is why he is so afraid!

The woman kept in contact with the social worker
She had fallen in love with this little boy.
She made arrangements to see him whenever possible
And when she did, she took him a special toy.

It was a ticket booth that read One Way Tickets To Heaven
She told the little boy, he could talk to Mommy and Daddy anytime.
All he had to do was take out his booth and they would see him
The little boy was so happy, you'd think he was on cloud nine.

Well, not all bad things that happen stay sad, you know
When God closes one door, there is always another one to open.
The woman adopted the little boy and loves him so
And a little boys heart is full of love, no longer torn and broken!

The Seed Of Love

A Story:

This is a story about two little angels, who were attending angel school in heaven
Their teacher called them aside, it's time for you to go to earth, instructions were given
But we are too small they cried, to be on our own
Their teacher replied, you are going to be with a little girl, who feels all alone!

Linda Laybolt
Whispers From Heaven

The Lord has asked that you go to be with her, the older angel said
He wants to see if you are learning all that in school,you have been taught and read!
The two little angels who had never been out of heaven, were somewhat afraid
When the older angel told them you are going today, plans have been made!

Within minutes the two little angels were on earth, standing inside a house
They looked around and there she was, the little girl who sat quietly as a mouse.
She looked at the angels and said, Hello my name is Cathy..Where did you come from?
The little angels were in shock, they wanted to hide and run!

They were not suppose to be seen by anyone, invisible to all
It was written in their angel instruction book, it was part of the angel law!
The little angels spoke up with big smiles on their faces, you can see us?
Cathy replied, Of course, I can, you are beautiful, what's the big fuss?

You're angels Cathy explained, I can see your wings behind you
She asked, Is it true that in heaven, everyone is happy, no one is sick and blue?
The angels replied yes, it's a very loving place that all embrace
And added, we even get to see Jesus, face to face!

Cathy got up holding something in her hand and said to them, come with me
They followed her to the back yard where a hole was dug for them to see
She got down on her knees,opened her hand which held a small seed
She threw it in the ground and said now you're not to grow into a weed!

Linda Laybolt
Whispers From Heaven

I planted the seed she said, one day it will grow to be a tree
It is suppose to remind me, how much my Mama loves me
She gave it to me last night, and said my home is in your heart and always will be
One day when you are older, the love in that tree, is all you will see!

Cathy smiled and covered the seed with ground, then proceeded to put water over it
My Mama made me promise, what she said, never to forget!
When the seed to sprout and grow, home I will be
I wish Mama would soon go home and take away the sadness from me!

For weeks the two little angels stayed close, by Cathy's side
For weeks she watered the seed, for weeks she cried
The little angels played, sang and talked about how beautiful was to comfort her
Cathy was so lost and full of sadness, for the loss of her dear precious Mother!

One day Cathy went out to check on her seed and there it stood
A tiny tree had peeked through the ground, just as her Mama said it would!
With joy in her heart, the tears flowed from her eyes
Mama is home! Mama is home! My heart no longer cries!

The little angels looked at her and replied, your Mama is not here
No, said Cathy but I know where she is and with you, I will share
Mama told me to go plant this seed, she called it the seed of love
And when it grew I would know, she is happy in her new home with God in heaven above!

The little angels stayed with Cathy for a few more days
They noticed she had changed so much, much more happier in her ways
When they returned to heaven, Cathy's mother greeted them with a smile
She said Thank you for being with my Cathy for awhile!

The little angels replied, we have a message to share with you
Cathy said to tell you, she loves you and is no longer blue!
She is happy you finally made it home and is no longer in pain
Her seed of love is now a tree, in her heart forever, it will remain!

The little angels teacher wrapped her wings lovingly around both with a huge smile
I am so happy you're back but it may be only for awhile!
You have both passed your first angel test away from here in heaven above
For you both understand, the Lord's Divine Words on The Seed Of Love!

The Heart When It Cries

A Story:

Two executives decided to go out and have lunch one day
Since they both worked for different companies, they decided to meet half-way.
The most expensive restaurant in town is where they agreed to meet
All the rich went there but the food was not that great to eat!

Linda Laybolt
Whispers From Heaven

Since the restaurant they were going to was only a block away from each other
They both decided to walk there and meet one another.
They were brothers but they were different as night and day
But they loved one another in every possible way!

While Jim, the younger brother, was walking to meet his older brother Jude
He saw an old man sitting on the sidewalk, begging for food.
He stopped and out of his pocket, he handed him fifty dollars in bills
Thank you Sir, he said, now I can buy some pills!

Jim started to walk away and then thought what a fool I have been
I just gave that man money for drugs so he turned around to look at the man again.
But he could not see him anywhere in sight
For an old man, he thought, he can move like the speed of light!

Then, he spotted him across the street talking to a woman
So over he walked to confront the old man.
As he approached he could hear the woman saying
You are so kind, this is truly a blessing!

Ya , Jim grumbled to himself, of course, you'd say he was kind
He just gave you fifty dollars for drugs, the man is out of his mind!
Just wait till I get you alone old man, I'm going to tell you a thing or two
Actually, having you arrested and thrown in jail is what I'd like to do!

Jim stood there waiting, with tears in her eyes, he heard the woman say
I feel terrible taking this as I know you have not eaten today.
You are an angel sent down from heaven above
She kissed the old mans cheek and added your heart is so full of love!

Linda Laybolt
Whispers From Heaven

The old man gave the woman a hug telling her to go to her little one
Make sure you get some food and pills for your sick little son.
Take my blanket with you, it's suppose to be colder tonight
And hopefully, he will be better by tomorrows daylight!

After Jim heard all this, he felt so terrible and torn up inside
That poor old man has a huge heart that is deep and wide.
I will get some food and another blanket for him
I know there has to be something, I can do for all of them!

Jim left and returned about three hours later, and looked for the old man
Finally, he spotted him and placed a hot bowl of soup in his hand.
When you have eaten this and are all warmed up, I want you to come with me
There's a place I have down the street, I want you to see!

The old man followed Jim but did not know where he was taking him to
This is my house said Jim, ,now it belongs to you.
I want you to go and get the woman and her sick little one
Everything in the house is there that you all need, including a bed for her little son!

The old man was in shock and tears filled his eyes
Jim said, I have to go now but I'll be back to see you, I live close by.
The old man kept thanking Jim as he walked out the door
Jim had a smile on his face but he wished he could have given him more!

As he walked up the street, he thought today is a day that I will forever behold
I met an angel in disguise and brought him in out of the cold!
But little did Jim realize that he was also an angel too, in disguise
For many cannot hear as he did in the old man, the heart when it cries!

Faith, Hope, Trust And Love

A Story:

Out in the country, down a long lonely road
Lived an old farmer who was extremely rude and bold.
An ole crank, he was called by all
No one went near him or beckoned to call!

One day, four angels landed at his door
When he saw them he yelled, "What did you come here for?"
Surprised, the four angels did not know what to say
As they starred at the man, who was old and fray!

The first angel Faith spoke up and said
We heard you were hungry, so we brought you some bread.
The old man laughed at the angels as they stood in his doorway
Be off with you all, use your wings and from here fly away!

The second angel Hope decided to speak
This bread is made especially for you, please, at least have a peek.
The old man grumbled some more
What is with you angels, Get away from my door!

The third angel Trust said, Sir, we are not leaving here
You can yell all you want but we won't disappear.
The Lord in heaven sent us to you
For a long time now, you have been lonely and blue!

The fourth angel Love added, We come here with love
Sent to you from our Lord, in heaven above.
He does not like the idea of you being alone living in such despair
So he sent us with this bread to let you know that he cares!

He has heard your cries within your heart
He sees that your whole world is falling apart.
So he sent the four of us to let you know
That he has always been with you, in everything that you sow!

Faith you have displayed in planting your seeds
Hope is that many people, your crops will feed
Trust is that your crops will get lots of warmth from the sun
Love is the care you put into them, like a loved one!

The angel Love handed the farmer the bread
Please take our Lord's gift, enjoy it as you are heavenly fed.
The old man looked at all four angels, with a smile on his face
And replied in a soft spoken voice, Thank you all for coming to my place!

The four angels decided now was time for them to depart
They could see that they had finally gotten to the old man's heart.
The old man took the bread, carefully unwrapping it with care
Instead of bread was a Bible and note ,Four angels was here bringing bread to share!

The Believer and The Atheist

John 15:13
Greater love hath no man than this, that a man lay down his life for his friends.

A Story:

In an old age home, two men laid in beds, side by side
Both were old, but still full of dignity and pride!
Once complete strangers, now the best of friends
Patiently waiting, for their lives to come to an end!

Every morning the believer looked up to the sky
And said, Thank You Lord, with tears in his eyes!
Closely, the atheist watched him but never said a word
Sometimes wondering if the believer was ever heard!

Linda Laybolt
Whispers From Heaven

All they had was each other to talk to, day in and day out
Both were bedridden, so it was impossible to move about!
They spent hours talking about days that were long gone by
Mostly about family and memories that met one minds eye!

The believer always talked about going home to Heaven
He had no worries, his sins had been forgiven!
He talked about the angels divine voices up above
And how His Saviour died for him, Out of Love!

The believer read his Bible everyday and gave Praise to the Lord
The atheist often drifted to sleep, from being so bored!
One day the believer got fed up with the atheist falling asleep
And decided to pray for his dear friend and started to profondly weep!

The atheist awoke to the sound of his friend crying
And thought to himself, Oh my, he must be dying!
He rang for the nurse to come, to see what was wrong
He was not ready to bid his friend farewell and say so long!

Without realizing it, the atheist started to pray
Don't take my friend, Dear Lord, instead take me today!
I know I haven't lived a righteous life, but he is a good man
He can do more good here for you, I know you understand!

So I'm begging you to take my life, let my dear friend live
I know it's too late for you to show me mercy and forgive!
Let my friend spread some more of your love around
I am a sinner and willing for him, to lay my life down!

The believer stopped crying and looked at his friend
He found this very difficult to even comprehend!
His friend was willingly ready to give up his life to save his
No greater friend can be found than this!

So all ended well, the atheist became a believer, at last
The atheist that once was, existed only in the past
The two old men spent the rest of their remaining days
Engulfed in the Lords Love, Forever, giving unto Him Praise!

The Angel Song

A Story:

Sitting alone in a church one Christmas Eve,
A little girl walked in and sat in two pews ahead of me
What happened next was to hard for me to believe
For a little angel from heaven, was all that I could see.

As she carefully got down on her knees
She put her little hands together, closing her eyes
And then she started to pray with such ease
Pouring out all her love for Jesus, for a heart never lies.

I'm sorry Jesus, I have no gift to bring
For you tomorrow on your special day
But I have a song to sing
I hope that it's ok.

I know I'm new up there
And perhaps, I should not have come here
But I know you always listen to all prayer
So I came to talk to you, my heart has something, I want to share.

The older angels sing with their divine voices to you
Many songs of praise and joy
I want to ask you, why can't we sing too?
We have lots of songs also for you, to truly enjoy.

They say we are too small to sing
For you are Our Mighty King
When we get older, we'll have our wings
Our voices will be heard, as our hearts joyfully sings.

They say we have alot of growing to do
Before we get to sing in front of you
So I came down here tonight
To sing to you, I hope that it's alright.

Linda Laybolt
Whispers From Heaven

Then the little girl stood up and turned around to face me
There was a man standing behind me with a smile upon his face
He nodded, that's when the little girls voice seemed to be set free
Tears filled my eyes, for she sang with so much beauty and grace.

Jesus, you love me, this I truly know
For your Holy Bible tells me so
My love for you is honest and true
In heaven, I always will stay, just to be with you.

For Jesus, you love all us little children
And, we love you too
Our love for you is in our hearts
And from you, we will never part.

Every night I get down on my knees
To you, who reigns in heaven above
A little prayer, I say to you
Sending it filled with love, sending it with love.

The little girl ran back towards the man
Jesus, did you like it? she said
I sang it as loud as I can
Yes, my dearest child, as you sang to me, a tear, I did shed.

Jesus, then picked the little girl up into his loving arms
Smiling at her, he said, tonight child, my heart truly sings
All of a sudden, a bright glowing light appeared on the little one
Turning around, all she could see was a small set of angel wings.

Angel wings, are they really mine to keep?
Yes, my dear little one, you will need them whenever you sing to me
But at the moment, it's time for us to go home and put you to sleep
Tomorrow, all heaven's children,will be able to sing to me and have wings, you'll see.

Linda Laybolt
Whispers From Heaven

As he walked by carrying the little angel, he smiled at me
Then he whispered, such a beautiful blessing, given to me tonight
The words of her song , in my heart will forever be
My dear little angel singing about her love for me on this Most Holy Night.

When they were gone, I sat there for the longest time
The voice of the little angel singing kept going through my mind
Her love for Jesus in her song sure did shine
For no deeper love is there, than that of a young child, will you ever find.

Jesus, you love me, this I know
For your Holy Bible tells me so
My love for you is honest and true
In heaven, I always will stay, just to be with you.

For Jesus, you love all us little children
And, we love you too
Our love for you is in our hearts
And from you, we will never part.

Every night I get down on my knees
To you, who reigns in heaven above
A little prayer, I say to you
Sending it with filled love, sending it with love.

God Is Everywhere

A Story:

One day, I decided I was going to find the one they call the Almighty
I had made my mind up, I wanted to meet he!
The people who walked with hearts of love, I wanted to be just like them
Thus, began my search for him!

Linda Laybolt
Whispers From Heaven

I'll go to church like some people do
Then, maybe God I will get lucky and see you!
So off to church I went, but sadly, I didn't see you there
But the pastor did say, God's presence was in the air!

I attended many churches but still no sign of you
I started to wonder if you're existence was really true!
So I decided to make a journey of my own
In search of God and His Mighty Throne!

I have all the time in the world for this
I want to see for myself that God is real and truly exists!
So off I went searching from place to place
For I really did want to meet, God face to face!

I climbed the highest mountains there is
But there was no sign of this heaven of his!
They say his throne is in heaven up above but where oh where
For I looked and looked and it was not there!

So I decided to sail the mighty seas
Maybe out there God, I will meet thee!
But again my excitement was soon taken away
So I had to think of another strategy for me to portray!

I traveled to God's largest churches, so vastly talked about
Seeing you had become my obsession, without any doubt!
So I decided to pack in and head back home
And have a little rest while thinking of more places to roam!

When I got home, heaven was the only thing on my mind
They say God is everywhere, but yet you are so hard to find!
Then, I picked up the Bible, reading the pages one by one
It took months but I couldn't put it down, till I was done!

Linda Laybolt
Whispers From Heaven

I learned so much from this book, for it touched my very soul
I'm a new person, renewed in God's love, complete and whole!
Now, I walk with love in my heart, like the others
My Lord taught me the true meaning of Love One another!

Heaven is the place where My Mighty Lord sits on his throne
Exactly where it is located, to me is still unknown!
My Lord Jesus is waiting for me there
With open arms,he will take me into His Loving Care!

Now I understand that Lord, you are everywhere
I was looking in all the wrong places, so unaware!
All I have to do is go to you in humble prayer
For my God in Heaven is always there!

A Penny For Your Thoughts

A Story:

An elderly homeless man was walking down the street
Suddenly, he saw a familiar face walking towards him on the sidewalk
He wore old shabby clothes and as he approached her
He waved for her to stop, saying could I have a moment of your time to talk?

He pulled a small brown paper bag out of his pocket
Then quickly handed it to her to hold unto
I know its not much, but it's all I have to give to you
I wish I could give more for all the kindness that you do!

The woman stood there smiling at the homeless man
What is in here she meekly asked, wondering to herself, what could it be?
Just take it home, it's a gift for you from me
There is a note attached for you to read, just open it, you'll see!

The woman smiled at the old man and gave him a hug
Thank you so much, this is a very kind thing that you have done
Have a good evening and keep warm tonight she said

Linda Laybolt
Whispers From Heaven

I'll read this as soon as I get home, sorry I have to run.

The woman placed the paper bag in her purse
It was starting to snow, she wanted to get home right away
She was tired tonight from the long day at work
Even though it was all volunteer work, she loved it anyway!

When she got home, she quickly prepared something to eat
Then checked her phone for any messages
Sitting down in her favorite chair, she reached for her favorite book
Opening her Bible, slowly she started to turn the pages.

A few hours had passed and the woman had fallen asleep
She woke up and decided it was time for bed
When she was walking by her purse, she thought of the brown paper bag
So she took it out and sit down to see what the note said.

Inside the bag was five pennies, each wrapped separately in plastic
Tears filled her eyes when she read what the old man had written on the note
It was one of the most precious gifts that she had ever received in her life
A lump formed in her throat, when she read what the old man had wrote.

There are exactly five pennies placed in this bag for you
You have been a dear friend to me and I will always love you!
These pennies I have held unto for years but now we must part
So I have decided to give them to you, with all my love from my heart.

So here is one penny for all your loving acts of kindness
One penny for every tear, for strangers that you have ever cried
One penny for every smile, you have generously given away
One penny for all the love, you share that you carry deep inside....

The last penny is very precious meant for only you, please do not forget
I call it my friendship penny and I want you to have it.
Where ever you go, take it with you my dear friend
For I will never ever have a true friend like you again!

Linda Laybolt
Whispers From Heaven

The woman sat for the longest time with tears in her eyes
What a sweet old man, what an angel he was full of love
The next day, she looked at the shelter for the old man
But soon discovered, He had departed and went Home last night
To Heaven Above!

So Help Me God....

A Story:

The young man was lead to the witness stand, where he was placed to sit
He was given a Bible and told to place his hand upon it
Do you swear to tell the whole truth and nothing but the truth, so help me God?
I do replied the young man with a solemn smile and a quick nod.

The young man was approximately 33 years old
Patiently, he sat waiting for his story to unfold
His hair was dark in color, shoulder length possibly dark brown
He looked like a hippy, no wonder he was the talk of the town!

All eyes in the courtroom were focused upon him, people whispering back and forth
No one really knew where he had come from, rumor had it somewhere up north
The prosecutor approached the young man and asked him to reveal his name
He answered with, My name is Trirhc Susej, but everyone calls me Drol from where I came!

The charges that have been laid are very serious, do you understand?
You have broken the constitution and all the laws of our land!
You have been accused of slander and treason, spreading things that you know nothing about
Would you like to change your plea before we start, and admit publically you are wrong beyond any doubt!

Linda Laybolt
Whispers From Heaven

The young man looked up with a smile on his face and replied, I do know what I say is true
I do not lie and I will speak the truth as I know it, unto all of you
I believe that I also have rights and must be allowed to speak, if that is ok
May I proceed without any interruptions, will you please listen to what I have to say?

The prosecutor nodded yes and proceeded to sit down as the man began to talk
Everyone was silent, the only thing that could be heard was the ticking of the old wooden clock
First of all, You had me swear on the Bible, so help me God
You swear in God's Name, yet to me this seems so very odd!

Every court in the country does the same thing, and I wonder why as this country does not believe
This makes me sad inside and my heart at times grieves
All your laws and constitution fall under God, so you say
Yet only few live their lives to following God's way!

You celebrate holidays throughout the year in God's name
Few really know what their meaning is, so who is at blame?
Sunday is suppose to be the Sabbath, the Lord's day of worship and rest
But in this country, its a day of Sunday shopping at its best!

You let young children starve and cry from hunger pains, how can this be
This so-called rich country, the so-called land of the free
You invest your money in wars and research to answers, that are already here
A Nation that has proven over and over again, that it just does not care!

You even have on your money, In God We Trust
Yet in reality there is no trust in God, which I think is slander and unjust!
You bring me to court with charges of slander and treason
Yet, this country and others are guilty of it, one by one!

Linda Laybolt
Whispers From Heaven

My Father is not pleased at all with the way things are going here
Nations need to change, it has to start somewhere
Mankind needs to return their trust and faith to the Lord in Heaven
When this happens, blessings upon nations will be given!

All in the courtroom started to clap and cheer out loud
The judge banged his hammer with force at the crowd
Then he ordered the young man to face him and stand
Announcing that all charges against him were dismissed, firsthand!

Then he told the young man, I appreciate what you had to say
But you have implied to God as your Father, and that is not really ok
It is one thing to speak your mind with freedom
But the day will come, your words will be judged from the higher kingdom!

The young man stood and asked, May I say something before I go?
The judged nodded yes and the young man said I have something to tell you, which I think you all should know!
As I stated, I do not lie, My name is Drol Susej Tsirhc, I am the Son
Spelled the correct way is Lord Jesus Christ, I am the One!

So you see, God is my Father who sent me here to you
To deliver his message starting here to go into world view!
As he spoke a bright light glowed all around Him, His work was done
Before, He disappeared a voice was heard saying "Well done, My Son!"

My Lord, I Thee Do Love....

A Story:

As I sat on my veranda, looking up towards the sky
My mind starts to wander, as the clouds softly stroll by.
If you look closely, many pictures can be portrayed
With a little imagination, so much is displayed!

Linda Laybolt
Whispers From Heaven

First, I saw what looked to be an angel with wings
Carrying a trumpet, was I really seeing these things?
Right behind her, I am sure it looked like more in full view
Embedded in the clouds, quietly passing through!

Wow, I thought this is unreal, angels in the clouds
No just one, but by the looks of it, in big crowds.
I carefully watched to see where they were bound
Secretly hoping they would see me and come down to the ground!

I wondered to myself, where they were all heading to
It must be an important place, I'd go to if I only knew
But sadly, the clouds whispered away with the breeze
The beautiful angels, come back to me please!

Feeling somewhat disappointed now, I decided to look up again
For the sky can be like an endless sea, of great domain
I'm glad I did as I could not believe my eyes
More clouds, more pictures, what a pleasant surprise!

This time I could see huge mountains sitting there
Even though, they were amongst the clouds, high in the air
I have never seen anything like these ones before
Standing tall and proud, for all to admire and adore!

Nestled in front of them stood a huge, giantic place
Full of splendor and glamour, that I wanted so badly to embrace
Just strolling by hidden in the clouds, full of grace
Was I actually seeing a glimpse of Heaven, before my face!

Then I noticed a huge set of gates, that were swung open so wide
I could see a man standing there waving, I bowed my head and cried
For I knew in my heart, it was the Lord Jesus, standing in Heaven above
Then I waved back to Him and shouted real loud," My Lord, I thee do love!"

The Swan

A Story:

One day a beautiful white swan was swimming gracefully in the pond
Her mate was never out of her sight as they held a very special bond
She watched as her mate drew closer to her with their young on his back
The male always carried them there encase of a predator attack.

Her surroundings were so peaceful and calm, just as she
There's no better life form than what the Lord has given me
I love this life of mine she sang out loud with emotion
And you my Lord will always have my devotion.

As her family drew close to the swan, she could hear her daughter say
Mama is singing extra loud to the Lord today
Mama says when she sings to the Lord, she feels all happy inside
And her love for him, she never will hide.

Just then a predator appeared and grabbed the father by the neck
Taking him under the water and the little ones fell off of the fathers deck
Into the water and down under they all went
None had learned how to swim yet, was so very evident.

The mother swan rushed over to save her little ones
She could not find her daughter but she found all of her sons
She placed them all on her back and took them to the shore
The predator was gone, so she and her mate searched for their daughter some more.

Giving up, sadly returning without their little daughter to the shore
The mother swan cried out, my baby is gone who I love and adore
Why Lord did you let this happen to me she screamed
As she swam away from her family, heading downstream.

Linda Laybolt
Whispers From Heaven

Suddenly, she thought she heard a little voice off in a distance
It seemed to be coming from her left where there was a small clearance
The closer she got to it, the louder the cries became
Mama, Mama, You heard me call your name!

The mother swan tears turned to tears of joy as she grabbed her little daughter
Swimming as fast as could back to her brothers and father
The mother swan started to shout; Lord, please forgive me
For not putting my faith, trust and love in thee!

Well, the Lord forgave the mother swan, for the rest of her days she live happily
Everyday she sang loud to the Lord, along with her family
A lesson can be learned from this story about the swan
Never lose faith, trust or love in the Lord, for he always listens when called upon!

Behold, A Child Is Born In Bethehem!

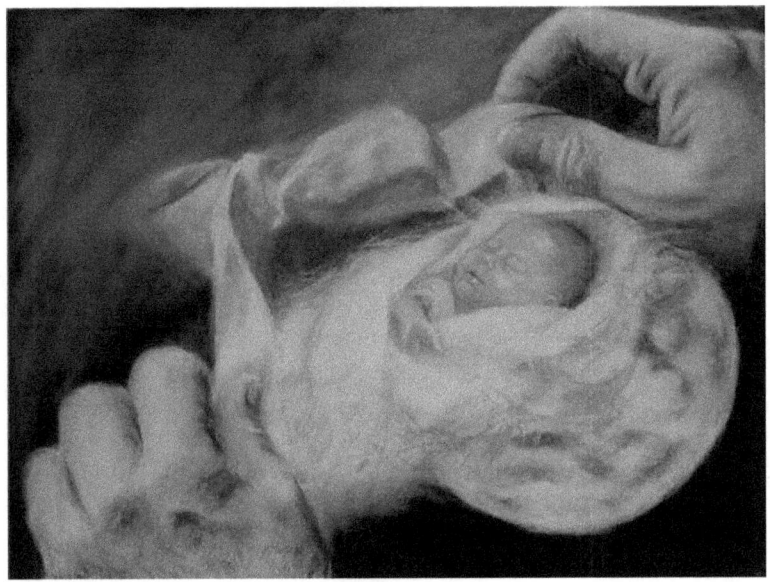

Outside tiny snowflakes started to fall upon the ground.
Visibility was poor, with the small gushes of wind.
Causing the snowflakes to float around!

It was Christmas Eve, all cheered with joy and relief! The news had just finished its last broadcast before Christmas. Everyone was in a huge rush to get home to their families, even though it was almost midnight!

Locking the door, he thought to himself, this is going to be a long night.
Have a Merry Christmas All, Jim shouted as everyone was heading out. Guess I should make some fresh coffee.

As he headed towards the coffee machine, he heard the fax machine printing.

He wondered what could be so important that there is news coming through
on Christmas Eve? I'll check it on my way back!

As he headed back to his office, the fax machine went off again. He went directly to it. The paper read Breaking News...Reports from Bethlehem that the Messiah was born in the early hours this morning. More updates to follow....

Well thought Jim...this is really a big prank! Someone has alot of time to waste tonight! Not to mention my time!

As Jim settled into his desk, he realized that it now the early morning hours of Christmas Day. He had no family so he always stayed to keep the station going on Christmas Eve and Christmas Day to let his employees spend their holidays with their families. He never liked Christmas anyway. He had been brought up in different foster homes so Christmas was not his favorite time of the year. For the last 17 years, he stayed at the station during Christmas.

He would catch a few hours sleep, here and there in the next couple of days. He had a little kitchen in his office stocked up with food so he was all set.
Once again, the fax machine went off....This time it read....Breaking News From Bethlehem....Shepherds Report Seeing Angels, Proclaiming that the Son Of God has been born to Mary and Joseph in Bethlehem. "THE MESSIAH HAS ARRIVED!" They were told to follow the bright shining star to find Him....More to follow...

Jim read it and laughed. Yes, he said out loud...The Messiah was born over 2000 years ago and His name was Baby Jesus! I'd like to know what idiot out there is sending these faxs! Once again, the fax machine started....Reports all over Egypt of a bright light shining in the sky...Scientists say it is a meteor close to earth, others claim...It was put there by God! Whatever is happening in Europe is affecting the planet worldwide! More Reports To Follow...

Linda Laybolt
Whispers From Heaven

As Jim settled down to his desk next to the fax machine, it occurred to him that he was being so stupid...sitting here waiting for another fax to come in. As if he did not know, what the next one was going to be! Old news, he thought....No one is interested in 2000 year old NEWS....Yet, he himself waited for the next fax!

And sure enough, here it was coming through! Breaking News....Three Kings From the Orient has just arrived in Bethlehem with Gifts To Offer the Newborn King! They are currently at a stall which animals are kept in, near an Inn located in Bethlehem. Could they have possibly found the baby Of Mary and Joseph! Live Reports say... "The Light From The Sky Is Shining Directly On The Stall!" Stay Tuned for more updates!

Well, this is keeping me wide awake, Jim thought. Oh well, I got nothing better to do! He turned on his computer and to his surprise, the faxes he was receiving was all over the internet news everywhere! Then, he decided he better turn on his television in his office....the same thing was being reported on all the stations. Reporters from all over the world are heading to Bethlehem!

What is going on here, Jim said out loud! Has the world gone crazy tonight? Just then, a News Breaking Report came on the television. The announcer had tears in his eyes...We are here reporting live in Bethlehem...History is being made as we speak...Thousands of people are standing behind me with hopes of getting a glimpse of Baby Jesus, who is inside this barn with His parents Mary and Joseph. Kings from the Orient just entered the building. All worldwide religious leaders are currently on their way to Bethlehem. Also, there is talk of all World Leaders to arrive here within the next 24 hours. Security is being sent from just about every nation around the world! We will point our cameras to the sky so you all can see the star that is shining on this building. Also, Angels can be seen everywhere...some singing and some playing trumpets and other musical instruments. It is truly amazing! He continued his broadcast with, Joseph and Mary is allowing our cameras to enter the building for only a few minutes but we have to be very quiet as Baby Jesus is sleeping...As he walked inside, there was Mary and Joseph with the Wise Men from the Orient, all kneeling beside the Manager. It was completely made out of straw and there He was Baby Jesus! His little body was wrapped in swaddles of cloth, which definitely was not fit for the Son of God! A Divine light shined upon His little head! Jim thought to himself, this is so Holy! He got down on his knees and bowed his head, then continued to watch. The cameras were allowed to get a close-up of Baby Jesus. The Newborn King was sound asleep. The camera turned to focus on all the animals in the building. They were all watching Baby Jesus, not one was making a sound. From in here, all that could be heard from the outside was the angels voices singing...Glory To All, In Heaven and Here On Earth! Then, the cameras turned and left the building. When he reached the outside, he ended his broadcast with...."What A Blessed Event This Is!....Hallelujah! To Our Majesty!...Baby Jesus!"

Wow! Jim said out loud. This is really big!...How come 2000 years ago when Baby Jesus was born there was not such a worldwide stir made?

I can't believe my eyes and ears! If I had not witnessed this for myself on Live TV, I would not have believed it! Baby Jesus, The Son Of God is here!
Just then, the phone rang waking Jim up! He had fallen asleep after settling into his desk with his coffee, which was now cold as ice. It was his secretary wishing him Merry Christmas! She said she would be over about 4pm with a big plate of turkey dinner. Jim thanked her for calling and wished her Merry Christmas! However, he announced, I will not be here later. I am heading home to shower and I am going to church today. His secretary was quite shocked! She had never known Jim to go to church in all the 17 years, she had worked for him. Then, she said...well drop over for dinner at 2. It's just the four of us here and we would love to have you join us. Thanking her, he said he would be honored to have Christmas Dinner with them saying, See you later!

When he hung up the phone, he sat back and thought of the dream he had, which was playing over and over in his mind. He could not get over how vivid his dream had been. It seemed so real at the time, not like any other dreams he had. Now, he completely understood what Christmas was all about!

Linda Laybolt
Whispers From Heaven

He got up and made some fresh coffee. I'll hang around here for about an hour, then I am out of here for the next couple of days, he thought. As he was walking by the fax machine, he noticed a piece of paper laying on the floor. He picked it up and read it, Breaking News..."Behold, A Child Is Born In Bethlehem!" Smiling, he said out loud...Indeed, There Was! "Baby Jesus! Hallelujah!"

www.ingramcontent.com/pod-product-compliance
Lightning Source LLC
Chambersburg PA
CBHW060821050426
42453CB00008B/529